The Pocket Essential

LAUREL & HARDY

www.pocketessentials.com

First published in Great Britain 2001 by Pocket Essentials, 18 Coleswood Road, Harpenden, Herts, AL5 1EQ

Distributed in the USA by Trafalgar Square Publishing, PO Box 257, Howe Hill Road, North Pomfret, Vermont 05053

A CIP catalogue record for this book is available from the British Library.

ISBN 1-903047-60-9

1 3 5 7 9 10 8 6 4 2

Book typeset by Pdunk
Printed and bound by Cox & Wyman

*To Cameron: may Stan and Ollie always raise your spirits, as
they do mine.*

Acknowledgements

Thanks to all those tireless researchers and fans who have dug into the history of Laurel and Hardy, especially John McCabe (the pioneer) and detail-oriented Randy Skretvedt and Glenn Mitchell. Also many thanks to Titan Books stalwarts Bob Kelly and David Barraclough for plugging the video gaps.

CONTENTS

1. Introduction: Mr Laurel And Mr Hardy

Laurel and Hardy. The names alone are enough to raise a smile. They made 106 films together, not always recognisable as the team that audiences would come to know and love. It's an amazing body of work, as much for its consistent quality as for the endless laughs the films contain. The characters of 'Stan and Ollie' whom Laurel and Hardy created as their screen personas have struck a chord with generation after generation of viewers, whether through cinema screenings, 8mm home movie releases, television screenings, video releases or newly-restored films on DVD. Every technology developed in the almost 80 years since Laurel and Hardy began making movies has featured them, including copious websites on the internet. Kids today still find the innocent slapstick, verbal dexterity and command of comedy of Laurel and Hardy hilariously funny. The Laurel and Hardy appreciation society, the Sons Of The Desert, has a long history and a huge international membership. All of this, of course, stems from the films and the films came from two very creative men.

Stan Laurel, the creative powerhouse behind the Laurel and Hardy films, started life as Arthur Stanley Jefferson. He was born in the Lancashire town of Ulverston on 16 June 1890. With a theatre-owning, vaudeville-performing father, Laurel's destiny was decided for him. From the moment he stepped on stage as a child in one of his father's productions, Laurel knew the show-business life was for him. After performing in vaudeville in the UK as a teenager, he sailed to the United States in 1910 as part of the Fred Karno troupe of performers alongside Charles Chaplin. From 1914 to 1922, Laurel toured American vaudeville theatres, developing his stagecraft and comic timing. During this time he partnered on stage and off (in a never-ratified common-law marriage) with Australian dancer Mae Charlotte Dahlberg Cuthbert. It was through Mae's discovery of a picture of a wreath of laurel that Arthur Stanley Jefferson came by his stage name of Stan Laurel. Their stormy relationship lasted until 1925, although Mae would resurface once Laurel found fame and fortune in the movies.

Stan Laurel started working in films in 1917, beginning with *Nuts In May*. He made over 60 solo films, often at the rate of one each week. It was an ideal training ground for a young man finding his way in the field of film comedy. From the beginning of his film career, Laurel took an active part in the writing and directing of his films for various Hollywood studios, learning the tricks of this newly developing art form on the job.

Also in Hollywood in the late 1910s and learning about the movie business was Oliver Norvell Hardy, known to all as Babe. Born 18 January, 1892, in Harlem, Georgia, Hardy grew up with his hotel-manager mother following the death of his father shortly after Hardy's birth. Music was Hardy's first love and aged eight he toured the American South as a boy soprano with a minstrel troupe. Sent to Atlanta to study music, Hardy instead got a job in a theatre singing to slides for 50¢ per day. By the age of 18 he was running the first movie theatre in Midgeville, Georgia. Annoyed by the bad acting he saw in the movies, he set off in 1913, aged 21, to Florida where there was a burgeoning movie business, determined that he could do better.

Indeed, he could. Between 1914 and 1917 Hardy appeared in over 100 film shorts, usually playing 'heavies' or villains (due to his size) in support of comic talents like Larry Semon and Billy West. Never having acted on stage, Hardy developed subtle film acting skills suitable for the big screen that many old vaudevillians lacked. Like Laurel, Hardy married young, to pianist Madelyn Saloshin in 1913. They were divorced by 1920, whereupon Hardy promptly married Myrtle Lee Reeves, a film actress he'd known from childhood. This was to be a turbulent marriage which, like Laurel's to Mae, would cause him problems in later years.

Hoping to develop his film career, Oliver Hardy went to Hollywood. There he met and worked with another young, struggling movie comedian, Stan Laurel. The pair featured in a 1920 short called *The Lucky Dog*, their first appearance in the same movie. It would be another seven years until they appeared together again, and several more years after that before they became the recognised team of Laurel and Hardy, but in that 1920 short the seeds of long-lasting comic greatness were sown.

2. The Silents: Before The Teaming, 1920-1927

The Lucky Dog

Producer Gilbert M Anderson. Director Jess Robbins. Two reels. Probably written & filmed December 1920 - January 1921. May have been released by Metro late 1921 - early 1922. With Florence Gillet

Story: A stray dog befriends Stan and helps him outwit a robber (Hardy) and a Swiss count (the robber in disguise). In between, he causes chaos at a dog show.

Production: The film had a mysterious history - it was assumed *The Lucky Dog* was made in 1917 because Stan Laurel said so in a 1950s interview. However, a 1920 California license plate spotted on a car and the established whereabouts of the primary cast members through 1917-20 suggest that *The Lucky Dog* was made in late 1920 or early 1921. Records of the distribution of the film are sketchy, due to the collapse of the production company, but *The Lucky Dog* seems to have enjoyed a brief release about a year after it was made.

Verdict: This obscure film is only notable for featuring Laurel and Hardy playing against each other, but like ships in the night they passed each other by and didn't appear on screen together for another seven years. 1/5

45 Minutes From Hollywood

Director Fred Guiol. Story Hal Roach. Two reels. Written & filmed circa late 1925, reshoots March-April 1926. Released December 1926. With Glenn Tryon, Charlotte Mineau, Theda Bara, Our Gang

Working Title: Her House Sheik

Story: A country boy, his sister and his grandfather travel to Hollywood to pay an outstanding mortgage where they encounter movie stars (but only those under contract to Hal Roach Studios, of course), are mistaken for bank robbers and cause havoc amid the guests and staff of a hotel, including the house detective (Hardy) and a 'starving actor' guest (Laurel).

Production: In 1925 Oliver Hardy was working as a contract player at the Roach Studios. Stan Laurel was also there as a writer, director and occasional performer. Since *The Lucky Dog* the pair had worked together at the Roach Studios, with Laurel co-directing Hardy as part of the cast of a trio of shorts: *Yes, Yes Nanette*; *Wandering Papas*; and *Madame Mystery*. During 1925-26 Roach began an all-star series of comedy shorts, each of which featured some or all of his top comic talent, including Laurel, Hardy, James Finlayson, Charlie Chase and Edna Marion. *45 Minutes From Hollywood* was the first Roach film to feature both Laurel and Hardy on screen, albeit not in the same scene together. Hal Roach would produce every major Laurel and Hardy film up to *Saps At Sea* in 1940.

Verdict: The pair never really work together. Hardy sports a toothbrush style moustache, while Laurel looks more like James Finlayson in his incongruous face fuzz (the result of a dispute between Laurel and his previous producer Joe Rock which prevented him from appearing in Roach's films). There are, though, some character traits which would become recognisable as Stan and Ollie's: there's Ollie's sheepish look to camera when caught out and Stan's ineffectual whimpering under duress. However, it is a long way from here to the Laurel and Hardy we'd later know and love. 1/5

Duck Soup

Director Fred Guiol. Story Arthur J Jefferson (Stan's father). Two reels. Written & filmed September-October 1926. Released by Pathé, March 1927. With Madeline Hurlock, William Austin, Bob Kortman

Story: To escape being recruited by the Forest Rangers, vagabonds Stan and Ollie hide out in the mansion of the vacationing Colonel Buckshot. When a pair of aristos enquire about renting the house, the boys pose as the owner and maid.

Production: Following Roach's instruction to keep writing himself into his short films, Laurel turned to a music-hall classic originally written and performed by his father (*Home For The Honeymoon*, 1908) for inspiration. Laurel remade it with sound in 1930 as *Another Fine Mess*.

Originally, the part of the second hobo was not earmarked for Hardy. Roach contract player Syd Crossley was to play the role, but for unknown reasons Crossley was out, Hardy was in and a classic comedy team was (almost) born.

The Stan and Ollie characters are costumed as generic hobos. In particular, Ollie wears a top hat rather than a bowler and sports a monocle and a heavily-stubbled chin. However, in character and actions, this features the Stan and Ollie audiences would later embrace: Ollie is bossy and in charge, while Stan is prepared to be led.

Although Laurel and Hardy would revert to playing different characters and simply appearing together in films again until *The Second Hundred Years*, it's clear from *Duck Soup* that they'd found a basis from which great things could develop.

Verdict: Made just one month after *45 Minutes From Hollywood*, *Duck Soup* is something of a revelation. Long lost, until a print was discovered in Belgium in 1974, it had been believed that the Laurel and Hardy partnership evolved gradually through the next half dozen or so shorts, but here it is almost fully formed. 3/5

Slipping Wives

Director Fred Guiol. Original Story Hal Roach. Two reels. Written & filmed October-November 1926. Released by Pathé, April 1927. With Priscilla Dean, Herbert Rawlinson, Albert Conti

Story: Stan is a deliveryman, hired by a spurned woman to make her neglectful artist husband jealous. Stan, confused between the husband and the family friend, makes a mess of the attempt, not helped by the family butler (Hardy).

Production: In another Roach's all-star short, this time featuring Dean and Rawlinson, one time dramatic stars who'd fallen on tougher times, Laurel and Hardy play the comic foils to these stars, not as a team in their own right. Stan and Ollie are antagonists who square off against each other. This short also features some ideas later expanded in *The Fixer-Uppers*.

Slapstick: When Stan calls at the house to make a delivery, he and Ollie end up rolling around on the floor in a fight which climaxes with Ollie covered in paint. Cue Hardy's trademark 'hurt dignity' look.

Verdict: Hardly vintage Laurel and Hardy. There's just too much thoughtless running around in the Mack Sennett tradition. 2/5

Love 'Em And Weep

Director Fred Guiol. Original Story Hal Roach. Two reels. Written & filmed November-December 1926, reshoots January 1927. Released by Pathé, June 1927. With James Finlayson, Mae Busch, Vivien Oakland, Charlie Hall

Working Title: Better Husbands Week

Story: An old flame (Mae Busch) of businessman Titus Tillsbury (James Finlayson) threatens to expose their past, destroying both his marriage and career. He sends his aide (Laurel) to keep her away from a dinner party he and his wife are hosting.

Production: Hal Roach's story for *Love 'Em And Weep* was developed by Laurel and the Roach Studios gag men. Laurel reused the premise in 1931 for *Chickens Come Home*. This version is notable because it features the first appearances of the three actors who were to become Laurel and Hardy's best-known co-stars: Finlayson, Busch and Hall. Australian-born Busch had enjoyed some success in dramatic movies, but by 1926 her career was on the wane after a dispute with MGM and a nervous breakdown. Her switch to comedy was inspired and she proved a worthy foil to Laurel and Hardy. James Finlayson was an expat Scot who'd started out as one of the Mack Sennett comedy troupe. He'd retained his fake comedy moustache from his Sennett days, and (along with his bald head) it was to become a trademark. Finlayson called himself 'Jimmy,' but was better known by the nickname 'Fin.' Finlayson's comedy trademark was his 'double take' (often noted in the Laurel and Hardy scripts as 'giving the one-eye'). The later short *Men O' War* (1929) features a series of six Finlayson double takes in a row. The butler in *Love 'Em And Weep* was Charlie Hall, known on the Roach Lot as "the Little Menace." He'd often pop up in Laurel and Hardy films as their nemesis. For much of this short Finlayson is the lead, with Laurel in support and Hardy as a visitor to Finlayson's home and witness to the chaos Mae Busch and Laurel unleash. Hardy is hidden behind a ridiculous moustache (again) and glasses. Even the on-screen billing separates Laurel and Hardy.

Slapstick: Stan is vigorously wrestled to the ground by Mae Busch who wants his car keys (the inspiration for a similar extended gag at the centre of *Way Out West*).

Verdict: This is minor stuff, only notable for developing Laurel's character. Compared with the remake (*Chickens Come Home*, 1931) in which Hardy plays the businessman and Finlayson is relegated to the butler role, *Love 'Em And Weep* is a weak entry lacking decent characters. 2/5

Why Girls Love Sailors

Writer & Director Fred Guiol. Two reels. Written & filmed January-February 1927. Released by Pathé, May 1927. With Anita Garvin, Malcolm Waite, Viola Richard

Story: Sailor Stan's fiancée is kidnapped by a gruff sea captain. Stan dresses in drag and romances the captain, whose philandering ways are exposed in front of both the captain's wife and Stan's fiancée. Ollie appears as the ship's second mate.

Production: Unseen for many years, *Why Girls Love Sailors* eventually resurfaced in the Cinémathèque Française in the mid-1980s. Although Laurel and Hardy play against one another, it does have Anita Garvin in her first Laurel and Hardy film. She'd later go on to be a regular, contributing to such classics as *From Soup To Nuts* and as the girl who falls on the custard pie at the climax of *The Battle Of The Century*. Interestingly, an early script draft has the boys working together much more like the characters audiences would later recognise, including a visit to a Chinese restaurant which features much confusion over the menu.

Slapstick: Stan (in drag) flirts with Ollie as the second mate, in order to reach the captain's quarters to rescue his sweetheart. As Ollie closes his eyes and puckers up for a kiss, Stan runs off.

Verdict: Mildly amusing, but occasionally tedious. 1/5

With Love And Hisses

Director Fred Guiol. Story Hal Roach. Two reels. Written & filmed March 1927. Released by Pathé, August 1927. With James Finlayson, Frank Brownlee, Chet Brandenberg, Anita Garvin, Eve Southern

Story: Stan is an army private, Finlayson the tough captain and Hardy the gruff sergeant in this almost plotless army comedy.

Production: Laurel and Hardy share more scenes but they are adversaries again. The army camp shoot took place near Griffith Park in LA. James Finlayson had to put up with wearing a pair of boots a size too small, hence his angry demeanour on screen.

Verdict: This is very amusing stuff, featuring many gags and situations which would be repeated in later (and better) Laurel and Hardy films, including the army-based feature *Pack Up Your Troubles*. The climax, with the platoon hiding behind a Cecil B DeMille billboard and being chased by angry wasps, is worth the price of admission alone, even if it prefigures the climax of *Bonnie Scotland*. 2/5

Sailors, Beware!

Directors Hal Roach & Hal Yates. Story Hal Roach. Two reels. Written & filmed April 1927. Released by Pathé, September 1927. With Anita Garvin, Harry Earles, Frank Brownlee, Lupe Velez

Story: Stan is an honest cab driver shanghaied aboard a cruise liner, where con artists Anita Garvin and her midget husband (who dresses as a baby) are working the passengers. Ollie is the purser on board the ship, and is responsible for keeping Stan busy.

Production: This film revealed the potential Laurel and Hardy had as a team. They share a few significant scenes together, during which the film comes alive. Hardy named *Sailors, Beware!* as being the one in which he developed his famous 'look to camera' and 'tie-twiddling' (actually missing from the final print) routines. Written and directed by Hal Roach (with one day of reshoots by Hal Yates), this film gave the studio boss a clearer idea of what he could do with the two men who were month by month, film by film emerging as his top comic talents. Actress Anita Garvin recalled: "*Sailors, Beware!* wasn't planned as a 'Laurel and Hardy' picture, but even I remarked to Stan how well they worked together as a team. This was the first inkling they had of pairing them: it just happened." *Sailors, Beware!* is also notable for a brief, but significant, poolside appearance by a young Lupe Velez, a Mexican actress who became a big star and who later featured with Laurel and Hardy in *Hollywood Party*.

Verdict: Except for the fact that Stan is much more self-assured and self-confident than his usual character would allow (witness his 'debate' with the ship's captain), both he and Ollie are showing clear characteristics that an audience today would recognise as quintessentially Laurel and Hardy. 3/5

Now I'll Tell One

Director James Parrot. Filmed April 1927. Released by Pathé, October 1927. Two reels. With Charlie Chase, Edna Marion, Lincoln Plummer, May Wallace, Will R Walling, Wilson Benge

Story: Divorce court comedy which sees a couple (Chase, Marion) engage in a series of tales (each illustrated) to discredit the other. Laurel plays Chase's hyperactive lawyer, while Hardy turns up as a policeman in one of the 'flashback' tales.

Production: This long-lost Charlie Chase two-reeler is not in most Laurel and Hardy filmographies because researchers were unaware they both appeared in it. Only reel two has been discovered, confirming the presence of Laurel and Hardy. It seems unlikely, given the structure of the story, that the pair shared any scenes in the first reel. The discovered footage was screened at the Stan Laurel Centennial in London, 1990, and has not been distributed commercially.

Do Detectives Think?

Director Fred Guiol. Story Hal Roach. Two reels. Written & filmed April-May 1927. Released by Pathé, July 1927. With James Finlayson, Noah Young, Frank Brownlee, Will Stanton

Story: The Throat Slasher killer (Young) vows revenge on a judge (Finlayson) for sentencing him to death, so the judge hires two private detectives (Laurel and Hardy) for protection. Arriving after a detour via a graveyard, the pair fail to realise that the killer has taken the place of the judge's new butler.

Production: Although shot in Spring 1927, this film was not released for some months because Roach cut his ties with distributor Pathé Exchange and switched to MGM, just as Laurel and Hardy began to become popular as a movie team. To maximise the few films they still had in stock to release, Pathé slowed down their release schedule. This is the first Laurel and Hardy film to feature Noah Young (a real-life champion wrestler) as a criminal (usually a comic, threatening murderer) and the whole scenario was revised to become the talkie *Going Bye-Bye*. Young had been featured in Harold Lloyd shorts since World War I. His character name, the Tipton Slasher, apparently derived from Lancashire folklore and may have been a tip of the hat from Laurel to his homeland.

Slapstick: Easily the best bit is the graveyard sequence (foreshadowing 1928's *Habeas Corpus*) which encapsulates so much of what would be recognised as classic Stan and Ollie, from the nature of the relationship to the facial expressions and even the business with the hats - which has a fine pay-off at the end of the picture.

Verdict: Still not an official team in the eyes of Hal Roach or those of contemporary movie audiences of the 1920s, Laurel and Hardy are here closer to their classic characters than ever before. Although augmented with the addition of detective accoutrements like badges and guns, this film marks the first appearance of the derbies and the traditional down-at-heel suits. Many think of *Do Detectives Think?* as the first true Laurel and Hardy film. 4/5

Flying Elephants

Directors Hal Roach & Frank Butler. Story Hal Roach. Two reels. Written & filmed May 1927. Released by Pathé, February 1928. With James Finlayson, Viola Richard, Dorothy Coburn

Working Titles: Were Women Always Wild? Do Cavemen Marry?

Story: Two cavemen, tough guy Ollie and winsome Stan, compete for the hand of the same cavegirl, Rose, daughter of toothache-suffering caveman James Finlayson.

Production: Laurel and Hardy are the stars of this film, but they play caveman enemies who only meet up in the final minutes so don't expect to find their Stan and Ollie characters here. Production took Roach and the crew to Moapa, Nevada, 60 miles north-east of Las Vegas, to capture a suitably prehistoric landscape. As with *Sailors, Beware!* it appears that Roach largely directed this effort, with the credited director (Frank Butler) merely helming one day of reshoots. The title comes from Ollie's comment to a cavegirl that "the elephants are flying south for the winter," a fact shown in animation. Animator Roy Seawright drew the airborne elephants and later contributed effects to such Roach productions as *Topper* and *One Million BC*. The film was at the centre of a distribution dispute between Pathé and Roach after Pathé began distributing Mack Sennett comedies in direct competition with Roach's own output. Roach switched to MGM and Pathé left *Flying Elephants* on the shelf for some months, only releasing the film when the growing popularity of Laurel and Hardy as a team was becoming clear.

Slapstick: James Finlayson, as a caveman suffering toothache, ties a rope to his tooth and the other end to a rock, which he then proceeds to throw over a cliff. Naturally, Fin goes over too, but at least his toothache is cured.

Verdict: A curiosity - this is one of the few films which sees Stan and Ollie out of contemporary clothes. 2/5

Sugar Daddies

Director Fred Guiol. Two reels. Written & filmed May-June 1927. Released by MGM, September 1927. With James Finlayson, Noah Young, Charlotte Mineau, Edna Marion

Story: Millionaire oilman James Finlayson marries after a night of drunken partying. In addition to a wife, he finds himself saddled with a gold-digging stepdaughter and brother-in-law. He hides out in a hotel with his lawyer (Laurel) and butler (Hardy), and escapes when Stan climbs on his shoulders, dons an extra-long coat, and pretends to be Ollie's rather tall wife.

Production: The final film before the official teaming, but the first under the MGM-Roach distribution deal, so the first to be billed as a 'Laurel and Hardy' comedy. Hardy is back to his butler character from *Slipping Wives* (with moustache intact), while Laurel, as the lawyer, plays his part much as he did in his many solo films before coming to Roach. Based on a two-page outline, originally Laurel was the Butler and Hardy was Finlayson's secretary. The climactic sequence of the film – and the only reason for paying it any attention today – was shot in the Pike Amusement Park in Long Beach. Here, with Laurel and Finlayson pretending to be an extremely tall and ungainly woman and Hardy as her escort, there is something of the emerging Laurel and Hardy magic. Watch for the young boy in these sequences, who was apparently following the camera crew around, and the bemused looks on the amusement park's patrons.

Verdict: Worth watching for the fun house and amusement park sequence, but little else. 2/5

3. The Silent Films: After the Teaming, 1927-1929

The Second Hundred Years

Supervised by Leo McCarey. Director Fred Guiol. Two reels. Written & filmed June 1927. Released by MGM, October 1927. With James Finlayson, Tiny Sandford, Ellinor Vanderveer

Story: Escaping from prison by posing as painters, Stan and Ollie paint the town white (literally), and escape a suspicious policeman by mugging a pair of visiting Frenchmen who are on their way to visit the prison they've just escaped from. Their ruse discovered, the boys are soon back behind bars.

Production: By June 1927, Laurel and Hardy had appeared together in 11 Hal Roach two-reel comedies, but no one had thought to make them a permanent film-making team. Director Leo McCarey (*The Awful Truth, Going My Way* and the Marx Brothers' *Duck Soup*) is the man credited with that inspired notion. McCarey started his film-making career in 1918 as assistant to Tod Browning (*Dracula, Freaks*). Throughout the 1920s, McCarey worked his way up through the ranks of the Hal Roach Studios, including a long period directing Charley Chase shorts, and by 1926 he was Vice-President in charge of comedy production. Enthusiastic about the possibilities of the Laurel and Hardy combination, he began supervising the production of their films starting with *The Second Hundred Years*. Until he left the Roach Studios in December 1928, he directed four of their comedies, contributed to the scripts of several others and personally supervised the production of them all. Next to Laurel and Roach, McCarey was the man most responsible for developing the unique Laurel and Hardy brand of comedy.

MGM began promoting the new team of 'Hardy and Laurel,' as they were called in the press sheets. They were even referred to as a 'new comedy trio' with James Finlayson included as a member of the team. The on-screen titles, however, billed the team as Laurel and Hardy, possibly at the insistence of Laurel, since he was the creative one, while Hardy much preferred golfing to the laborious work of scripting gags.

Surprisingly, Stan Laurel wasn't keen on the idea of being in a team. He wanted to return to the writing and directing role which had first brought him to Roach. However, the chance to control the Laurel and Hardy pictures, to really be writer/director in all but name, convinced Laurel to stick with the teaming. For his part, Hardy was delighted with this development. Apart from the regular work involved, he was thrilled to be one of the leads in a new comedy series, a big step up from his days as a movie 'heavy.' This was director Fred Guiol's last Laurel and Hardy film: he'd directed practically all their Roach films to this point.

Slapstick: During the painting spree, Stan inadvertently applies his paint-laden brush to the posterior of a passing woman (Dorothy Coburn).

Verdict: This is the first 'official' Laurel and Hardy team-up film, although *Duck Soup* had given the boys their characters and *Do Detectives Think?* had given them their 'look.' Hal Roach and the two comedians were now beginning to think in terms of being a comedy team, and this shows in their characters, even if the shaved heads and prison clothes are an atypical look. As a comedy, *The Second Hundred Years* is a minor entry in the Laurel and Hardy catalogue. 2/5

Call Of The Cuckoos

Director Clyde Bruckman. Two reels. Written & filmed June 1927. Released by MGM, October 1927. With Max Davidson, Lillian Elliot, Spec O'Donnell, Charlie Chase, James Finlayson, Charlie Hall

Story: Max Davidson and his family are annoyed by the loony antics of their next-door neighbours (Laurel, Hardy, Finlayson, Chase and Hall). They move to a new house which immediately starts self-destructing, and find the same neighbours have just moved in next door.

Production: While waiting for the hair on their shaved heads to grow back, the following week Laurel and Hardy played second fiddle to Jewish comedian Max Davidson in a story that aimed to promote the Roach stable of comedians. Their scenes have a home movie feel to them, as they mug for the camera and engage in lunatic hi-jinks. This was director Clyde Bruckman's first work with Laurel and Hardy, making for a rather inauspicious start to his association with the team.

Verdict: There's little to recommend this guest appearance. The comedy might raise a smile, but it's not Laurel and Hardy. 1/5

Hat's Off

Director by Hal Yates. Two reels. Written & filmed August 1927. Released by MGM, November 1927. With James Finlayson, Anita Garvin, Dorothy Coburn

Working Title: Rough On Hats

Story: Washing machine salesmen Stan and Ollie attempt to deliver one of their machines to a house atop a huge flight of steps. A scuffle develops between them and they start trashing each other's hats. Soon, passers-by are drawn into the mêlée, and the scene becomes a hat-tearing free-for-all.

Production: Randy Skretvedt, author of *Laurel And Hardy: The Magic Behind The Movies*, called *Hat's Off*: 'The Holy Grail of Laurel and Hardy movies.' In 1927, this was the most popular of the duo's films, but now no known prints or even sections of this film are known to exist, even in private collections. This is especially annoying as the film seems to contain the genesis for the Oscar-winning Laurel and Hardy short *The Music Box* (1932) in which the washing machine is replaced by a piano. It also appears to feature the most extreme version of the classic 'mixed-up hats' routine.

Laurel came up with the idea for this short after he and his wife Lois were visited by a very persistent washing machine salesman. The trek up the lengthy flight of stairs came about when one of the Roach gag writers spotted the distinctive location at Vendome Street in the Silver Lake area of Los Angeles.

A Laurel trademark inadvertently stemmed from around this time. As his hair grew back during the weeks following *The Second Hundred Years*, Stan had a difficult time getting his regrowing hair to behave. Others found his unruly hair hilariously funny, so he decided to keep it as a permanent trademark.

Realising from his decreasing screen time that he wasn't set to be a star, James Finlayson walked off the lot after the filming of *Hat's Off*, only to return to regular Roach supporting appearances by the middle of the following year.

Verdict: Who knows – it could be a long lost classic... The reviews at the time were great, with the *LA Times* calling *Hat's Off* 'uproariously funny,' while the *LA Evening Herald* noted that '...it is no exaggeration to say that the entire audience bordered on hysteria at the climax... Hal Roach has the most promising comedy team on the screen today in Laurel and Hardy.' Rumours continue to circulate of a copy of the film in a private collector's hands in France, but no one has ever come forward.

Putting Pants On Philip

Director Clyde Bruckman. Two reels. Written & filmed September 1927. Released by MGM, December 1927. With Harvey Clark, Dorothy Coburn, Sam Lufkin

Story: Millionaire Uncle Mumblethunder (Hardy) goes to the docks to meet his Scottish, kilt-wearing nephew, Philip (Laurel). Mumblethunder does all he can to avoid being seen with Philip as they walk the streets and he draws crowds due to his strange attire. Philip is also obsessed with women and is easily distracted upon sight of a skirt: although he fixates on one woman in particular (Coburn). There's only one solution: Philip must be put in trousers!

Production: Laurel and Hardy abandoned their down-on-their-luck personas to play nephew and uncle in this brilliant short comedy. This short is more a fascinating commentary on gender roles in the 1920s than a typical Laurel and Hardy comedy. Stan is feminised more than usual: crowds gather to see this man-in-a-skirt, yet he's aggressively chasing vampishly-dressed Dorothy Coburn. Ollie's solution to the problem is to put Stan in trousers ('pants'). However, the encounter with the tailor who tries to measure Stan's inside leg leaves the Scot feeling affronted and ashamed at his treatment. Laurel drew some of his characterisation from his early solo short film *Short Kilts* (1924).

Verdict: Anticipating *The Seven Year Itch* (1955) and Marilyn Monroe by many years, Stan's kilt blows up around his legs when he walks over an air vent in the street. The same thing happens after he's lost his underwear, and assorted women spectators faint at the sight! This is most definitely atypical Laurel and

Hardy – and it's all the more amusing for that. By far the most hilarious of their early 'out-of-character' shorts. 4/5

The Battle Of The Century

Director Clyde Bruckman. Two reels. Written & filmed September-October 1927. Released by MGM, December 1927. With Noah Young, Sam Lufkin, Eugene Pallette, Anita Garvin, Charlie Hall

Story: Stan is a prizefighter, Ollie his trainer-manager. In his first fight, Stan is knocked out cold and ends up sleeping comfortably on the canvas. Ollie takes out an insurance policy on Stan, then attempts to stage an accident to collect on it. An encounter with a pie delivery man (Charlie Hall, who also appears in the crowd in the boxing sequence behind a ridiculous moustache) and a banana skin lead to a massive, citywide pie fight – reputed to be the largest in cinema history.

Production: Following the September 1927 'Fight of the Century' title fight between Jack Dempsey and Gene Tunney, Stan Laurel set out to make a boxing two-reeler. With only enough material to fill one reel, he did not know how to extend the gag. Laurel fell back on an old standby of silent film comedy: the pie fight. However, if Laurel and Hardy were going to do a pie fight, it had to be the most extravagant and spectacular pie fight ever committed to film. For Hal Roach, this was the film which convinced him that Laurel and Hardy could be the next big thing. "I believe that within a year they will rank with Lloyd, Chaplin and other comic geniuses," he claimed.

Regarded as a classic of silent comedy, thanks to its use of over 4,000 real pies in the battle (an entire day's output from the Los Angeles Pie Company), over half the footage from *The Battle Of The Century* was missing for years. Anita Garvin remembered of the shooting that "all those cream pies attracted bees. Seemed like there were thousands of bees buzzing around the pies as the day wore on. Some of those extras went home early they were so scared."

When producer Robert Youngson edited the pie-fight sequence for use in his 1965 compilation *Laurel And Hardy's Laughing 20s*, he was unaware that he was using the only existing – and rapidly decomposing – negative as his source. He managed to preserve a classic five-minute sequence, and it is on this sequence that the film's reputation was built. It was not until the early 1980s that a print of the first reel, the boxing sequence, was discovered. Still missing is footage from reel two in which Ollie attempts to take out a life insurance policy on Stan and then stages an accident with a banana skin: this leads directly into the pie fight. Video and DVD releases of this short cover the gap with title cards, script extracts and stills.

Look out for Lou Costello in the boxing ring crowd, just to the right of Oliver Hardy, long before his later fame as one half of Abbot and Costello 13 years later. In the 1950s Abbot and Costello would shoot their television show on the Roach lot, using scripts written by Clyde Bruckman (who later killed himself in a Santa Monica cafe using a gun borrowed from Buster Keaton). Bruckman recycled many of the old Laurel and Hardy gags for the new duo. If it was good enough for Stan Laurel...

Slapstick: The pie fight climaxes with Anita Garvin sitting on a pie thrown by Stan and trying to maintain a dignified exit...

Verdict: A comedy of two halves: the boxing sequence is simply a rough draft which would be more developed in *Any Old Port*, while the pie fighting sequence is the ultimate example of a joke which was old even in 1927. The trick here is that Laurel makes every pie count and gets a laugh from each one. This is no mere free-for-all, but a carefully choreographed series of gags, each building on the preceding one. It was a technique Laurel learned from the hat destruction in *Hat's Off*, and one he'd continue to build on throughout Laurel and Hardy's golden years in the 1930s. 4/5

Leave 'Em Laughing

Director Clyde Bruckman. Two reels. Written & filmed November 1927. Released by MGM, January 1928. With Edgar Kennedy, Charlie Hall, Viola Richard, Dorothy Coburn

Working Title: A Little Laughing Gas

Story: Stan has toothache so he reluctantly visits the dentist. After a mix-up in which Ollie has a tooth extracted, the boys overdose on laughing gas. They wreak havoc in their Model-T Ford through the streets of Culver City, drawing the ire of short-tempered traffic cop Edgar Kennedy.

Production: Leo McCarey came up with the idea for Stan to visit the dentist, a scenario reused in the feature film *Pardon Us*, almost unchanged. *Leave 'Em Laughing* was a rich source for later Laurel and Hardy films: the boarding house sequence was revived for *They Go Boom*, while the crazy driving of the conclusion was to be repeated at the climax of *County Hospital*.

Leave 'Em Laughing saw the first appearance of Laurel and Hardy's trusty mode of transport, the Model-T Ford. Nicknamed the 'Tin Lizzie,' Laurel claimed that all the autos featured in their films were built especially, particularly the stunt cars. "We had one in a half circle that would go around and around, and then one that was squashed between two cars... We had one that was all fitted together and you pulled wires – everything collapsed at one time."

Edgar Kennedy also made his Laurel and Hardy debut. He was often typecast as a figure of authority, like a frustrated policeman. Although only on the Roach lot for a short time, Kennedy directed two of the next three Laurel and Hardy shorts.

Verdict: Perhaps the first of the Laurel and Hardy shorts which feels like a genuine Laurel and Hardy film as they'd generally be recognised. There's the domestic set-up, the fear of an otherwise ordinary situation (a trip to the dentist)

and an anarchic climax. If that climax is a little lame compared to some of the classics, it just goes to show that it's still early days for the team. 3/5

The Finishing Touch

Director Clyde Bruckman. Two reels. Written & filmed December 1927. Released by MGM, February 1928. With Edgar Kennedy, Sam Lufkin, Dorothy Coburn

Story: Employed to finish off the building of a new house, Stan and Ollie fall foul of a nurse (Dorothy Coburn) from the adjacent hospital who wants them to keep the noise down and a curious cop (Edgar Kennedy), who is fascinated by the boys bizarre antics. Having finally finished, a cartoon sparrow puts paid to all their hard work, while their own van provides 'The Finishing Touch.'

Production: This film has its roots in Laurel's 1924 short *Smithy* (in which he is accidentally put in charge of completing an unfinished house, only to cause its collapse at the climax) and Hardy's *Stick Around.* Giving the boys an occupation related to the comedy that would follow created the template for future Laurel and Hardy shorts.

In the original scenario, quiet was needed at the hospital because the inmates were being driven mad by the noise of the construction site. Originally, the nurse was to be male, which is why she's so handy with her fists, using them against Stan, Ollie and Edgar Kennedy indiscriminately. Almost accidentally, Laurel and Hardy had hit upon the idea of the 'aggressive woman,' who was to become central to many of the later films.

The prop house was built by Roach's set construction gang on a vacant area of land on Motor Avenue, near Fox Studios in LA. Originally, the destruction of the house was to be caused by Stan and Ollie's car passing straight through it, leaving a car-shaped hole. However, the construction crew missed this instructions when building the house shell, so the car got stuck inside the building. Laurel decided the gag was funnier that way.

For a silent movie, much of *The Finishing Touch* depends upon sound: the boys are asked to work quietly and so tiptoe around and Stan rips sandpaper to trick the nurse into thinking her dress has torn. It's as though Laurel and Hardy were preparing for the arrival of sound: *The Jazz Singer* had opened two months earlier in October 1927.

The gag which sees Stan appear to be carrying both ends of a very long plank of wood was to resurface much later in *Great Guns.*

Slapstick: Stan searching for his lost bucket (which is hanging behind him on the back of his shovel) is priceless.

Verdict: If *Leave 'Em Laughing* gave us Laurel and Hardy's recognisable domestic situation, then *The Finishing Touch* finally gave them a job. It would be a format that would be repeated by the duo in infinite variations: the boys try their best to do a simple task, but end up making a bad situation much worse, but much funnier, too. For that reason alone, this is a seminal Laurel and Hardy short. Oh, and it has every wooden plank silent movie joke in the book! 3/5

From Soup To Nuts

Director Edgar Kennedy. Two reels. Written & filmed December 1927-January 1928. Released March 1928. With Anita Garvin, Tiny Sandford, Edna Marion, Ellinor Vanderveer

Story: A newly-rich couple (Garvin and Sandford) make the mistake of hiring Stan and Ollie as waiters for the important social occasion of their first dinner party. Having worked in railroad catering, the pair are more adept at spilling things than serving them. The diner comes to an unexpected climax when Stan is asked to serve the salad "undressed," and does so!

Production: As 1927 drew to a close, Laurel and Hardy were being recognised as a new comedy team by audiences who were flocking to see *Hat's Off* and *Putting Pants On Philip*. Coming up for release at the end of the year was the boxing and pie-fight epic, *The Battle Of The Century*. Additionally, Stan had just become a father as his wife Lois gave birth to Lois Jr. on 10 December 1927.

The director was E Livingston Kennedy, better known as Edgar. Like Laurel, Kennedy was as adept behind the camera as he was in front of it. Director of photography George Stevens (later an acclaimed director) sat this film out, allowing his place to be taken by Len Powers. Despite these changes, there was something familiar about some of the gags in *From Soup To Nuts*: Anita Garvin chasing a cherry around her plate was a straight lift from Laurel doing the same gag in *The Second Hundred Years* a few months before. This film itself was cannibalised by Laurel for the opening sequence in the extended version of *A Chump At Oxford*.

The climax may have been very different, too. A still exists showing gorgeous Anita Garvin without her dress, which has somehow found its way onto Stan. This alternative ending was shot, but discarded by Laurel who stuck with the sight of Ollie falling into a cake... for the third time.

Slapstick: When Ollie's hat falls in the soup toureen, it's a killer.

Verdict: This is another first draft, not only for *A Chump At Oxford* but many of the food-related gags which peppered Laurel and Hardy's comedies. While Hardy almost has his character down pat, especially his long attempt to recover his dignity after his first encounter with a cake, Laurel still seems unsure. Stan veers from childlike behaviour to aggressive shouting at the guests, fascination with Anita Garvin's behind and cruel neglect when he covers his eyes as Ollie heads for another slip on the pesky banana skin. He hadn't settled on his more childlike persona, but he was getting there. 3/5

You're Darn Tootin'

Director Edgar Kennedy. Two reels. Written & filmed January 1928. Released April 1928. With Otto Lederer, Agnes Steele, Christian Frank, Chet Brandenberg

Working Title: The Music Blasters (used on the UK release)

Story: Fired from a band after ruining a concert, Stan and Ollie are unable to pay for 14 weeks back rent and are evicted from their lodgings. They fare no better trying to raise funds by playing music in the street, falling foul of a cop, a drunk and their old bandmaster. Finally, they turn on each other. Instrument destruction turns to shin kicking and finally an orgy of trouser-ripping, which spreads through the passers-by.

Production: At the start of 1928, Roach, McCarey, Laurel and Hardy were much surer of who the 'Stan' and 'Ollie' characters could be. They'd tried out different looks, formats and techniques and were now able to settle on a series of conventions which would work and give the films a uniformity: the Laurel and Hardy films began to feel like a series. The down-on-their-luck, unable-to-afford-rent yet ever-trying journeymen that were Stan and Ollie had arrived to stay.

It took 10 days in total to shoot *You're Darn Tootin'*: three days on the bandstand sequences; five days on the Roach lot New York street set; two days shooting the middle boarding-house scenes.

Stan's unfastening of the salt and pepper pots during dinner in the boarding house was reused in *The Hoose-Gow*.

Slapstick: The trouser-ripping scene is often acclaimed as the best of the large-scale street battles from the Laurel and Hardy shorts.

Verdict: Dull and boring for the first reel (the bandstand section), this livens up no end with the final sequence. However, this tit-for-tat humour of destruction is not enough to elevate this short above the merely ordinary. 2/5

Their Purple Moment

Director James Parrott. Written & filmed February 1928. Released by MGM, May 1928. With Anita Garvin, Kay Deslys, Tiny Sandford, Fay Holderness

Story: Henpecked Stan and Ollie have been secretly saving for a night on the town away from the wives. When Stan's wife discovers the scheme, she replaces Stan's hidden loot with cigar coupons. The boys are unable to settle a huge restaurant bill, and their evening ends in a pie-throwing brawl in the restaurant's kitchen.

Production: This was the first Laurel and Hardy film to be directed by James Parrott, the brother of Charley Chase. Parrott would be behind the camera for many of the best Laurel and Hardy shorts until 1933, and he continued to write for the team until 1938. Of all the films to this point, *Their Purple Moment* is the most easily recognised as a traditional Laurel and Hardy short. It has the domineering wives and the co-dependent characters of Stan and Ollie.

Laurel and Hardy were now a successful comedy team, with the final quarter of 1927 being the best yet for Roach Studios, largely due to the new distribution deal through MGM. Laurel was earning $500 each week, while Hardy enjoyed a raise from $300 to $400 per week. Only 'supervisor' Leo McCarey, however, was actually earning a percentage of the films' profits.

Stan and Ollie still have silly character names, but in one scene Ollie can be clearly lip-read calling his pal 'Stan.' Also, upon discovering he has no money in his wallet, only coupons, Stan's face has an extraordinary serious look for a moment, before he adopts the usual crying pantomime. Much of the basic 'boys-escape-the-wives' plot would be reused in the feature-length *Sons Of The Desert*.

The original climax of *Their Purple Moment* ended up on the cutting-room floor, including an extensive sequence featuring the midget troupe of the Al G Barnes Circus. Scenes in which Stan and Ollie pretend to be members of the midget troupe performing in The Pink Pup nightclub were dumped after previews. The Laurel-written pie fight and tit-for-tat escalation in the restaurant kitchen was shot as a replacement. Hal Roach wasn't that impressed with the replacement scenes: "The business with the pies may not have been great, but that always worked with audiences."

Slapstick: Stan repeatedly falls on Kay Deslys in a suggestive manner.

Verdict: This is classic Laurel and Hardy. It is interesting to see so many elements, which would not fully emerge until the sound shorts of the 1930s, being tried out here in a rudimentary form. *The New York Daily Mirror* noted: "*Their Purple Moment* is a classic of the slapstick school." 4/5

Should Married Men Go Home?

Director James Parrott. Two reels. Written & filmed March-May 1928. Released by MGM, September 1928. With Edgar Kennedy, Kay Deslys, Edna Marion, Viola Richard, Charlie Hall

Working Title: Follow Through

Story: Ollie and his wife are enjoying a quiet Sunday at home when Stan visits, eager to play golf. After Stan wrecks much of the house, Mrs Hardy chases the boys out. At the golf course, they partner a pair of beautiful girls to complete a foursome. The girls want to be treated to sodas, but the boys are short of money. Stan leaves his watch to settle the 30¢ bill. On the course, they tangle with Edgar Kennedy and wind up in a mud-throwing battle.

Production: Shot just before the annual month-long shutdown of the Roach studios in April, *Should Married Men Go Home?* was the first film to be released under the distinct 'Laurel and Hardy' banner. Roach spent the holiday negotiating the 1928-29 line-up of comedies with distributors and owners on the cinema circuit, and returned with the clear message that Laurel and Hardy could play as a top-billed comedy team in their own right.

Ex-boxer and one of the original Keystone Kops, Edgar Kennedy was back in front of the camera. One of the biggest laughs in the film comes when he ends up with a divot on his head instead of his ill-fitting hairpiece.

George Stevens, who photographed many of the Laurel and Hardy shorts, recalled fondly: "That was the old style of comedy. Sometimes with Laurel and Hardy the story wasn't always there, but they'd keep trying things, changing things. The structure may not be linear, but that never mattered at Roach if the audience laughed. Every preview we had on that one, audiences laughed. That was such a reward with those two guys, hearing audiences rock with laughter."

Golf was a favourite sport of Oliver Hardy. As Laurel wrote to Ray Atherton in 1963, "Babe was social, he had his hobbies. We happily went our separate ways between pictures. He usually went to the Lakeside Golf Club. He didn't care to be involved in the preparation of our pictures." Hardy was often the winner of the annual Roach Studios Golf Tournament, usually held during the April shutdown of the studio. Ironically enough, in *Should Married Men Go Home?* Hardy doesn't actually get to take a swing at a ball!

Verdict: Much of this, minus the golfing action, formed the basis for *Men O' War* as well as inspiring part of *Come Clean*. Standing alone, however, this is a poorly structured series of physical gags, lacking any of the character material that would later come to be associated with top-notch Laurel and Hardy shorts. 2/5

Early To Bed

Director Emmett J Flynn. Two reels. Written & filmed May-June 1928. Released by MGM, October 1928.

Story: Ollie inherits a fortune from a deceased uncle, buys a mansion and makes Stan his butler. After a night of indulgence, Ollie returns home intent on playing a series of cruel practical jokes on Stan. Stan retaliates by breaking nearly everything in the house and threatening to quit.

Production: Other than *Brats* (in which they double as their own children), this is the only film to feature Laurel and Hardy as the only cast members. It's a shame that it is such an atypical example of their work. The comedians play a totally different relationship (that of master and servant) than the one they had been developing.

Director Emmett J Flynn, who'd made the original 1921 version of *A Connecticut Yankee In King Arthur's Court*, failed to impress either the stars or Leo McCarey, who had to arrange significant reshooting to finish the film satisfactorily.

Verdict: The whole thing seems misconceived: Ollie's pranks on Stan are simply cruel rather than funny and Stan's orgy of destruction has no comic pay-off. Only the business at the climax with the hideous fountain actually works, and even then it goes on too long. The action doesn't grow from the characters or their situations and the violence lacks the tit-for-tat element which would become central to so much of the Laurel and Hardy brand of comedy. A curiosity. 1/5

Two Tars

Director James Parrott. Two reels. Written & filmed June-July 1928. Released by MGM, November 1928. With Thelma Hill, Ruby Blaine, Edgar Kennedy, Charlie Hall

Working Title: Two Tough Tars

Story: Stan and Ollie are two sailors on shore leave. Hiring a car, they pick up two girls and spend the afternoon driving in the country. Caught up in a huge traffic jam, tempers boil over and soon the street is a mess of mangled cars.

Production: This comedy featured what Stan Laurel termed as 'reciprocal destruction,' with hats, pies, rocks, mud and trousers replaced by cars. If wrecking one car is funny, went Laurel's logic, why not wreck dozens? The trick here was that Laurel and Hardy slowed the pace of the destruction. In previous shorts, it has functioned as the climax to the movie, an ideal moment to fade out. Here, there was a slow build-up as each entanglement leads to the next, even more extreme, example of wanton vandalism.

Roach construction worker Thomas Benton Roberts built many of the 'breakaway' cars used in *Two Tars* and other Laurel and Hardy films. He and many other Roach employees feature in the film: they were all encouraged to bring their own cars to the shooting to serve as background. Roberts also featured in the film as an irate tomato-throwing motorist. Director James Parrott and assistant director Lloyd French controlled the car-wrecking action from horseback, riding up and down, shouting instructions through megaphones. Parrott also appears in the film, as the sunglasses-wearing motorist.

Slapstick: Stan gets his finger stuck in a chewing gum machine, and soon everyone is rolling around on the scattered gumballs.

Verdict: A true classic. *Two Tars* often ties with *Big Business* among Laurel and Hardy fans as the best of the duo's silent movies. Contemporary audiences thought the film so funny there is a least one report of the evening's feature film being postponed so *Two Tars* could be run again. A model of slow build comedy, *Two Tars* is a fine example of the silent movie short at its best. 4/5

Habeas Corpus

Director James Parrott. Two reels. Written & filmed July 1928. Released by MGM, December 1928. With Richard Carle, Charlie Rogers

Story: Stan and Ollie are hired by a mad scientist to steal a corpse from a cemetery. The scientist's butler, really a detective in disguise, follows the boys and thwarts their efforts – by frightening them.

Production: The first of Laurel and Hardy's macabre dark humour films (see also *The Laurel-Hardy Murder Case*, *The Live Ghost* and *Oliver The Eighth*), *Habeas Corpus* plays like a spin-off from the graveyard scenes in *Do Detectives Think?*

Habeas Corpus was shot entirely at night during the middle of July 1928 and went through much revision. A climax which sees Stan and Ollie return to the professor's house with their graveyard goods was cut, but exists in still photos.

Between the shooting and release of *Habeas Corpus*, the demand from cinemas for sound films was growing, and many silent subjects were beefed up with music and sound effects tracks. Film editor Richard Currier was charged by Hal Roach with adding these sound effects and *Habeas Corpus* was billed as Laurel and Hardy's 'first sound picture,' although there is no speech recording in it. The Vitaphone soundtrack was long lost, until a chance rediscovery lead to the 1999 release of the film complete with the original soundtrack on DVD. Making impressive use of Saint-Saens' *Danse Macabre*, the synchronisation of the sound effects definitely adds value to the film.

Slapstick: Stan climbs up Ollie to get over the cemetery wall. Ollie goes straight through the wall instead of over it.

Verdict: While containing some good gags, *Habeas Corpus* suffers from a lack of logic. What's the mad scientist all about? Well, he wants to try out a brain transplant, but that was cut from the script so there's no explanation in the film. Why does the detective-cum-butler decide to scare Stan rather than arrest him or send him on his way? Who knows! A minor entry, but a sign of bigger (and scarier) things to come... 2/5

We Faw Down

Director Leo McCarey. Two reels. Written & filmed August-September 1928. Released by MGM, December 1928. With Bess Flowers, Vivien Oakland, Kay Deslys

Story: Stan and Ollie sneak off to a poker game, telling their suspicious wives that they have a business engagement at the Orpheum Theatre. En route, they stop to help two women with a flat tire and wind up splattered with mud. The girls invite them up to their apartment to dry their clothes, and all proceed to get roaring drunk. When one of the girl's boyfriends returns, Stan and Ollie climb out the back window, in full view of their passing wives.

Production: The original idea came from Oliver Hardy, one of the few times he contributed creatively behind the scenes. He drew the basics of the tale from gossip he heard from his laundress.

After editing, the film was about 10 minutes too long, so Laurel and Leo McCarey cut one of the funniest sequences, in which Stan and Ollie, wearing the wrong trousers, repeatedly walk through newly laid cement, much to the consternation of a workman. However, Laurel hated to lose good comedy material, so he built the following film *Liberty* around some of the excised scenes from *We Faw Down*.

The final scene, in which gunfire results in many more men jumping from windows with their trousers around their ankles, is familiar from the Robert Youngson compilation *The Golden Age Of Comedy* and is also identical to the final shot of the Laurel and Hardy feature *Block-Heads*.

Slapstick: Stan's facial contortions and the 'making whoopee' scene are fun.

Verdict: Nothing to rave about, *We Faw Down* is mildly amusing. The central conceit of Stan and Ollie sneaking off to an event without their wives and being unaware that their cover story has been overtaken by tragedy was reused in the feature film *Sons Of The Desert*. 3/5

Liberty

Director Leo McCarey. Two reels. Written September, 1928. Filmed October-November 1928. Released by MGM, January 1929. With James Finlayson, Jack Hill, Jean Harlow

Story: Stan and Ollie escape prison and end up in the wrong trousers. Every attempt to switch clothes leads them into further trouble. A cop chases them to a construction site, where they escape by hitching a lift on an elevator to the top floor of an unfinished building. Atop the girders, 20 stories in the air, they finally switch trousers, contend with a crab that has found its way into Ollie's pants, and narrowly avoid falling to the ground several times.

Production: Stan Laurel and Leo McCarey wrote a framing story to use the trouser-swapping material cut from *We Faw Down*.

Anyone watching *Liberty* today makes the assumption that all the perilous climbing around on top of the unfinished skyscraper was achieved through special effects and Laurel and Hardy were in no real danger. This couldn't be further from the truth. That's why the backdrops of Los Angeles look so authentic: it's the real thing, not process work or back-projection, techniques which were only being developed in the late 1920s.

To film these sequences, the Roach construction team commandeered the top of the Western Costume Building in South Broadway, Los Angeles. The building was chosen for the accessibility of the roof and for the views it offered over LA. On top of it was built the girder framework upon which Laurel and Hardy clambered for real. Although the girders were actually made of wood, and the structure was only three stories high on the roof and not the 20 it appeared to be, it was still a dangerous way of making a film. Hardy took at least one tumble from the structure, falling 20 feet and receiving a few bruises. Most of the skyscraper material was included in the Robert Youngson compilation *Laurel And Hardy's Laughing 20s.*

This was the first film James Finlayson had made with Laurel and Hardy following his absence after a billing and pay dispute with Roach. The woman surprised when Stan and Ollie leave the back of a cab where they've been trying to change trousers was Harlean McGrew II, later better known as Jean Harlow, who got a five-year contract with Roach at the end of 1928.

Verdict: Fantastic stuff, *Liberty* is unique among Laurel and Hardy films because it puts the pair in such danger. This kind of thing was a staple of silent comedy shorts, but they often traded more off the danger, whereas (true to form) Laurel and Hardy's skyscraper exploits are rooted in their characters. 4/5

Wrong Again

Director Leo McCarey. Two reels. Written & filmed November-December 1928. Released by MGM, January 1929. With Del Henderson, Josephine Crowell, Harry Bernard, Sam Lufkin

Working Title: Just The Reverse

Story: Working as stablehands, Stan and Ollie overhear that "the valuable Blue Boy" has been stolen. Thinking that it's the horse of the same name (not the Gainsborough painting that's actually being discussed), they set out to return the animal to its millionaire owner. At the mansion, they are told to put Blue Boy atop the piano, which they attempt. After the horse runs wild through a few rooms, they are able to lure him on the piano, nearly crushing Ollie in the process.

Production: The idea for the confusion of a Gainsborough painting for a horse of the same name came to director Leo McCarey during a trip to the dentist where he saw a print of the *Blue Boy* painting.

The material with the horse and the piano was shot first, which is just as well as it turned out to be something of a struggle and it took a week to get the sequence on film to everyone's satisfaction. At the end of November, the opening scenes were shot at the Uplifters Club, a Los Angeles sports venue, which doubled for the stables.

Verdict: The *Blue Boy* misunderstanding is classic Laurel and Hardy, and is again an example of their comedy anticipating sound: it's a gag you really need to hear for it to work properly. Oddly enough, the film continues after the exit of Stan and Ollie, one of the few that doesn't involve the stars at the climax. 3/5

That's My Wife

Director Lloyd French. Two reels. Written & filmed December 1928. Released by MGM, March 1929. With Vivien Oakland, William Courtright, Charlie Hall, Jimmy Aubrey

Story: Ollie is set to inherit a fortune from a rich uncle. The catch is he must be happily married and his wife has just left, thanks to permanent house guest Stan. Now Stan must pretend to be Ollie's wife to convince the visiting uncle that all is well in the Hardy household. So good is his masquerade that Stan attracts the attention of a drunk at the Pink Pup nightclub. A crooked waiter and a stolen necklace serve to uncover the ruse and lose Ollie his fortune.

Production: The knock-on effect of the extended shooting period for *Liberty* meant that the last couple of films of 1928 suffered from abbreviated schedules as they had to be wrapped before the studio converted to sound at the end of the year. *That's My Wife* and *Big Business* were both shot very quickly during December 1928, with the first taking just six days to shoot.

Anticipating sound films, this short again boasts a wonderful Vitaphone music and effects track which adds considerably to what is a minor effort. At a cost of over $3,500 the discs were recorded in Camden, New Jersey by the Victor Corporation and featured George Olsen and his Orchestra contributing the score.

Verdict: The Stan-in-drag routine hadn't been used for several years, and it was employed to great effect here. Finally, the infamous Pink Pup nightclub is named in a dialogue intertitle. 2/5

Big Business

Director James Horne. Two reels. Written & filmed December 1928. Released by MGM, April 1929. With James Finlayson, Tiny Sandford, Lyle Tayo

Story: Selling Christmas trees door-to-door, Stan and Ollie encounter James Finlayson, managing to engage him in an escalating tit-for-tat war. Stan and Ollie find ever-ingenious ways of destroying Finlayson's home and belongings, while Fin sets to work destroying the boys' car. A bemused policeman looks on before intervening.

Production: Christmas week 1928 saw the circus of destruction descend on the Cheviot Hills area of Los Angeles, where a Roach location scout had secured permission to destroy a house. Roach claimed for many years that the film crew set up at the wrong house, but according to Laurel (in a letter to a fan) Roach's instinct for showmanship had got the better of him.

The other long-standing myth about *Big Business* was that Stan and Ollie had so much trouble selling Christmas trees because the film was set during summertime. That's clearly not the case: the film was shot Christmas 1928 (albeit in the Californian sunshine), features Stan and Ollie in thick overcoats and gloves and sees them wish James Finlayson "Merry Christmas" at the end.

This was the last Laurel and Hardy film which Leo McCarey worked on. He quit Roach in January 1929 to pursue a feature film directing career (the Marx Brothers' *Duck Soup*, among others). Despite this, he remained credited on the films up to *Hog Wild*, suggesting he'd left a fund of gags and story ideas behind.

The film exists in two distinct versions, in which the same action is seen from different angles. This was because many of the Laurel and Hardy silent shorts were shot twice, or with two cameras, in order to provide two negatives. One was for domestic US distribution and one for foreign screenings. As film negative duping technology improved, the need for double negatives became less, although many of the sound films were shot twice or more to incorporate foreign languages.

Acclaimed as a masterpiece, *Big Business* is one of only 100 films to have been placed on a list of American cinema classics by the Library of Congress.

Verdict: Proof that pressure of time can work in your creative favour, unlike *That's My Wife*. *Big Business* is probably the best-known of all the Laurel and Hardy silents. It draws upon and condenses two years of craft into a perfect short of reciprocal destruction. The cleverness lies in the way that (at least to start with) the vandalism of house and car is proportionate: Jimmy Finlayson rips the door off the car, Stan and Ollie rip the door off his house, and so on. 5/5

Double Whoopee

Director Lewis Foster. Two reels. Written & filmed February 1929. Released by MGM, May 1929. With Jean Harlow, William Gillespie, Charlie Rogers, Tiny Sandford

Story: As temporary doormen at a posh hotel, Stan and Ollie manage to drop a foreign Prince down an elevator shaft (several times), and cause offence or injury to hotel guests, hotel employees, cops and cab drivers, as well as finding time to tear off Jean Harlow's dress.

Production: This is best known for the sight of the then 17-year-old Jean Harlow in her underwear. One story has it that there was even more of Harlow visible on the first take - a piece of film history which has not been restored. If the Prince reminds viewers of famed silent era actor/director Erich Von Stroheim, that's because the part was played by Von Stroheim's stand-in double, Captain John Peters. The short was an attempt to spoof the Von Stroheim film *Foolish Wives*.

Roach Studios closed for the month of January 1929 for the installation of the much-anticipated sound-recording equipment. It would take until March for it to be fully installed and working. Meanwhile, production of silents continued, even though all involved knew their days were numbered.

Although still credited to the now-departed Leo McCarey, much of the story came from Laurel, who now took full control of the Laurel and Hardy gag machine.

In 1969 a sound version of *Double Whoopee* was prepared (but not released until 2000). Using lip-readers to determine the actual on-screen dialogue, Laurel and Hardy fans and impersonators Al Kilgore and Chuck McCann created a 'talkie' from the silent original. While not entirely convincing, this production does much to show that Laurel and Hardy were practically working as sound comedians long before the technology caught up with them.

Verdict: The reputation of *Double Whoopee* is entirely down to Jean Harlow's scene-stealing entrance. The rest of the film is amusing enough, and seems an odd choice for the faux-sound treatment. 3/5

Bacon Grabbers

Director Lewis Foster. Two reels. Written & filmed February 1929. Released by MGM, October 1929. With Edgar Kennedy, Jean Harlow, Harry Bernard

Story: Stan and Ollie, working for the Sheriff, are charged with serving a summons to Mr Kennedy (Edgar Kennedy) for non-payment of instalments for a radio. Easier said than done, the duo destroy both their car and the radio in the process, as a delighted Mrs Kennedy (Jean Harlow) comes home to announce she's just paid the final instalment...

Production: Shot in the final week of February 1929, the camera crew returned to the Cheviot Hills district of Los Angeles for the process-serving scenes, while the opening with Charlie Hall as the truck driver was shot on the Roach lot. This scene was originally longer, with Hall persuading Stan and Ollie to plug a radiator leak using rice, which later foams up into an expanded mush. Stills also exist showing Stan and Ollie in bizarre fake beards as they pretend to be the 'Smith brothers' in attempt to get close enough to Edgar Kennedy to give him the legal papers.

This and the following and final silent short, *Angora Love*, were released after the first handful of Laurel and Hardy sound shorts had reached cinemas. They were put out almost as an afterthought, complete with music solely performed by Le Roy Shield on an organ and some synchronised sound effects instead of the orchestras of previous scores. *Bacon Gabbers* was rescued from decomposition in the late 1960s when it was transferred to safety film. Even so, it is a rarely seen Laurel and Hardy silent.

Verdict: Interesting for being overlooked, *Bacon Grabbers* is a riff on the *Big Business* fight, but more subdued. The opening in the Sheriff office is reused in *Beau Hunks*. 2/5

Angora Love

Director Lewis Foster. Two reels. Written & filmed March 1929. Released by MGM, December 1929. With Edgar Kennedy, Charlie Hall

Story: An escaped goat attaches itself to Stan, follows him and Ollie home. Attempting to hide the animal in their apartment they can't help but attract the attention of their unhappy landlord (Kennedy).

Production: The final silent film is a first draft of *Laughing Gravy*. Some of the routines found their way into *The Chimp, Be Big* (the clothes-hanging scene) and *Beau Hunks* (the foot massage scene). Stills exist of what may be an excised scene as Stan and Ollie search for the goat in the foyer of a movie house staffed by cameraman George Stevens, although it is possible these were only gag photos.

Despite being released after many of the first Laurel and Hardy talkies, *Angora Love* did win some critical acclaim at a time when silent films were largely ignored. *Angora Love* was "sizzling over with rapid-fire, laughter-stirring situations" which caused audiences to be "all tied up in knots of laughter" according to a review in *Film Daily*.

Verdict: The last of the silent Laurel and Hardy shorts is amusing enough. More importantly, everything here is familiar, from the characters' attire (whether out in the world or at home) to their personalities and their domestic setting. All this would return, bigger, better and noisier with the coming of sound. 2/5

4. The Sound Shorts, 1929

Unaccustomed As We Are

Director Lewis Foster. Two reels. Written & filmed March-April 1929. Released by MGM, May 1929. With Mae Busch, Thelma Todd, Edgar Kennedy

Working Title: Their Last Word

Story: Ollie brings Stan home for dinner, which is enough to drive away his wife (Mae Busch, her first film with Laurel and Hardy since *Love 'Em And Weep*). Neighbour Mrs Kennedy (Thelma Todd) offers to cook for them, only to have her dress set on fire. Clad only in her underwear, she's hidden in a trunk as her cop husband (Edgar Kennedy) and Ollie's wife come home. Aware they have a woman in the trunk, but unaware it's his wife, Kennedy boasts of his own female conquests.

Production: Laurel and Hardy's first all-talking film... and boy, do we know it. From the overlapping dialogue of the argument between Mr and Mrs Hardy to the final joke (Stan falling down the stairs) which depends solely on sound, we are clearly into a new era in film-making. The technology was still primitive (the sound equipment would pick up the camera noise) and sound-editing techniques were still in their infancy, so cameras couldn't move. What was recorded live on set was pretty much what was used as the film soundtrack.

However, there were no silent comedians in Hollywood more suited to the coming of sound than Laurel and Hardy. For the best part of 1928, many of their silent shorts made no concessions to the lack of sound, and would have played just as well with dialogue. It was with sound, though, that their childlike characters were really crystallised. Hardy's Southern charm and Laurel's childish whimpering only really came across with the addition of sound.

Laurel knew that the Mack Sennett fast-paced pantomime slapstick would not be enough to sustain even a two-reeler in the sound format. Now, clever dialogue was going to be more important than messy pratfalls. He also had a more personal concern: "I had a kind of lisp at the time..." Laurel told an interviewer in 1957. Despite his concern about this and his English accent, both would go on to become among the more endearing traits of Stan. Hardy had no worries, as an eloquent speaker and singer, he couldn't wait to begin work on his first talking picture.

So important was a successful transition to sound films that Hal Roach got personally involved in supervising production once again (he drafted the initial scenario for this short) and he chose Laurel and Hardy to be the first comedy team on the Roach lot to make a sound short. At Easter 1929, four fixed cameras locked in soundproof booths began turning on *Unaccustomed As We Are*. There was only one set of sound-recording equipment so shooting took place through the night to accommodate an Our Gang comedy entitled *Small Talk* - it had to shoot during the day when the Our Gang kids could work.

Clearly, Laurel had been thinking carefully about the coming of sound and several gags depend on it, such as Mae Busch's nagging of Ollie taking on the rhythm of the record and the various off-screen sound effects and noises used to convey action. Reshooting and recutting (despite the added difficulty of editing a soundtrack) would continue to be the way Laurel honed the comedies to ensure that each was as laugh-packed as possible. Roach realised that audiences couldn't wait to hear Laurel and Hardy speak so rushed *Unaccustomed As We Are* into cinemas in early May 1929, ahead of the final three silent productions. As a concession to those cinemas which had not yet installed sound equipment, a silent version of *Unaccustomed As We Are* was also produced, boasting the most intertitles in any Laurel and Hardy film due to the increased dialogue (there were also silent versions of *Berth Marks* and *Brats*).

Classic Dialogue: Ollie's plaintive cry for help ("Why don't you do something to help me?") makes its debut in this short.

L&H Moments: Stan cries not once but twice, making this a weepie as well as a talkie.

Verdict: The voices of Stan Laurel and Oliver Hardy – what they said as well as what they did – would become integral to their comedy from here on, allowing the pair to avoid the career-ending encounter with sound of so many of their contemporaries. *Unaccustomed As We Are* gave Laurel and Hardy a new lease of life. 3/5

Berth Marks

Director Lewis Foster. Two reels. Written & filmed April 1929. Released by MGM, June 1929. With Harry Bernard, Charlie Hall, Baldwin Cooke

Story: Stan and Ollie are musicians, travelling by train to their next gig. They spend most of the trip trying to change into pyjamas and get comfortable just in time to arrive and disembark in their underclothes, minus their fiddle.

Production: The idea for *Berth Marks* allegedly came from Laurel recalling his vaudeville days spent travelling from venue to venue by the cheapest (and often most uncomfortable) way possible. The upper-berth scenes where the pair get tangled up took three days to shoot, mainly due to the fact that they kept cracking up during filming. Hardy's solution to a laughter attack was to go play a round of golf.

Most of the dialogue was improvised on the spot. As during the silent days, Laurel and Hardy worked without a dialogue script, only an outline of the general situation. This was one working habit they would rapidly change, as Laurel came to realise the importance of sharp dialogue to the sound comedies.

Laurel and Hardy were able to shoot their first location sound material at Santa Fe Rail Depot. A large crowd gathered to watch the filming.

L&H Moments: The hat-swapping routine appears for the first time in the sound shorts.

Verdict: Definitely a prime example of Laurel and Hardy taking a simple situation (catching a train) and making a 20-minute meal out of it. The clothing entanglements are worth the price of admission alone. 4/5

Men O' War

Director Lewis Foster. Two reels. Written & filmed May 1929. Released by MGM, June 1929. With James Finlayson, Anne Cornwall, Gloria Greer, Charlie Hall

Story: Stan and Ollie are sailors who hook up with two girls in the park. They treat the girls to sodas, though they haven't enough money for four. Stan wins a slot machine jackpot, enabling all to take a boat ride, leading to a boating battle.

Production: Drawing on *Two Tars* for the sailors concept and on *Should Married Men Go Home?* for the soda routine (vastly improved here), *Men O' War* follows the three-act structure of the Laurel and Hardy silent shorts closely, but would simply not have been the same film without dialogue. The entire opening sequence, including the double entendre about the gloves/underwear, relies on the spoken word.

Classic Dialogue: "They faw down," says Ollie, holding up some ladies underwear which dropped from a washing basket but he believes belongs to one of the girls. Instructed to drink half, Stan gulps all of Ollie's soda. "My half was on the bottom," he tearfully explains.

Verdict: Great location feel to this one, with the boys and girls having boating fun in the park. It shows how quickly Laurel and Hardy overcame the technical limitations of the new sound equipment and continued to make films their way: darn funnily! 4/5

The Hollywood Revue Of 1929

Producer Harry Rapf. Director Charles F Reisner. Dialogue by Al Boasberg & Robert E Hopkins. 120 minutes, black & white with colour sequences. Written & filmed Spring 1929. Laurel & Hardy signed 1 June, 1929. Released 21 June 1929 in Los Angeles; 23 November 1929 nationwide USA. With Jack Benny, Joan Crawford, John Gilbert, Cliff Edwards, Buster Keaton

Story: Stan and Ollie perform as magicians in a celebration of Hollywood's stars of 1929, but Stan's ineptitude keeps ruining the tricks, resulting in MC Jack Benny getting covered in icing.

Production: This film was made to give song and dance routines to silent Hollywood actors like Joan Crawford and Jack Benny. Laurel and Hardy were a late addition when it was realised that the two-hour production had next to no comedy in it, other than Buster Keaton in a cod-Egyptian routine. Hence, the all-star Technicolor rendition of *Singin' In The Rain* at the climax is notable for their absence.

The nature of the magic sketch and static style of the camerawork betrays the haste with which Laurel and Hardy's contribution to this Hollywood celebration was put together. It's similar to the kind of material Laurel would use for the pair's later stage appearances. Their appearance comes about 40 minutes into the film and lasts for only around six minutes.

Ironically, this guest appearance is the first Oscar nomination for Laurel and Hardy. The film was up for Best Picture 1928-1929, but lost out to *Broadway Melody*.

Verdict: Not really a genuine Laurel and Hardy film, it is a shame that the pair didn't have longer to concoct a better contribution to this celebration of film talent. Nonetheless, it showed how popular with audiences and important to the Hollywood film-making community Laurel and Hardy had become. 1/5

Perfect Day

Director James Parrott. Two reels. Written & filmed June 1929. Released by MGM, August 1929. With Edgar Kennedy, Kay Deslys, Isabelle Keith

Working Title: Step On It

Story: A planned picnic in the country with their wives and 'Uncle Edgar' doesn't get very far with Stan and Ollie organising things. They repeatedly destroy the sandwiches, inflict painful indignities on Edgar's gouty foot and have trouble with a flat tire, not to mention the neighbours. They eventually make it a block from home, where their car sinks into a huge mud hole.

Production: Laurel had witnessed a neighbour's endless preparations for a picnic and suggested to the Roach gag men that he and Hardy should set out for a picnic but never actually get there. The result was *Perfect Day*.

The neighbour with the window trouble was played by Baldwin Cooke, once a vaudeville partner of Laurel. He turns up in 30 Laurel and Hardy films in various bit parts. He was more prominent in *Perfect Day* for the simple fact that filming took place at his house at Vera Avenue in Culver City. The local mounted police were called in to keep crowds out of microphone range, and in a lesson learned from filming *Men O' War* shooting wrapped at 3pm each day to avoid attracting gangs of curious school children.

Laurel and Hardy director Lewis Foster, who'd overseen the conversion to sound, was transferred to Roach's Harry Langdon series in June 1929, so veteran James Parrott returned to direct for the first time since 1928's *Habeas Corpus*.

The final gag, where the car and all its occupants vanish into a mud hole in the middle of the street was achieved through mechanical engineering and great perseverance by the stars. The hole was dug in a street on the Roach lot and the car lowered in on a pulley system. The actors and actresses all had to put up with being dunked in the water, but it was worth it for the sight of all five hats, including two distinctive bowlers, floating on the surface.

L&H Moments: That moment just before Stan proceeds to toss a brick through the neighbour's window, Stan and Ollie look at each other with knowing glances, as if to say: "Here we go again!"

Verdict: The third sound classics. Their inability to organise themselves and achieve even the simplest thing is as evident as ever... 4/5

They Go Boom

Director James Parrott. Two reels. Written & filmed June-July 1929. Released by MGM, September 1929. With Charlie Hall, Sam Lufkin

Working Titles: Coughing Up, The Sniffles.

Story: Ollie has a bad cold, made much worse by Stan's best-intentioned efforts to look after him.

Production: This was shot and edited in five days before the annual Roach Studios month-long shutdown in August. Five days of shooting in a flannel nightshirt took its toll on Laurel, who told a reporter: "I feel like going home, getting dressed and going to bed." The climax, featuring the exploding air mattress, was the only tricky part of the shoot. Safety prevented a real explosion, so the mattress was inflated with air (not gas!) and three marksmen (a carpenter, a prop man and a film editor) shot at the mattress, causing the explosion effect.

During shooting, Hardy's wife Myrtle filed for divorce, accusing him of having affairs. They reconciled, but Hardy's marriage remained a stormy one. There was better news in the Roach accounts office, where the 11 silent films of the 1928-29 period had grossed a profit of $35,000, while the five sound shorts released to date had accrued $43,000 in profit as a result of the higher rentals charged and increasing cinema audience.

Classic Dialogue: "I'll pudding you in a minute," says Ollie, rather obliquely.

L&H Moments: Ollie's look to camera when Stan tears a hole in his nightshirt is priceless, while the inflated Ollie is one of the first examples of the pair using special effects in the sound films.

Verdict: Oddly enough, it seems more stilted and limited than the other sound shorts. 3/5

The Hoose-Gow

Director James Parrott. Two reels. Written & filmed August-September 1929. Released by MGM, November 1929. With Tiny Sandford, James Finlayson, Dick Sutherland, Ellinor Vanderveer

Story: Wrongfully arrested (or so they claim), Stan and Ollie end up on a chain gang. Ordered to gather wood in exchange for lunch, the boys cut down a tree, unaware that it contains a watchtower with a guard on duty. The Governor (Finlayson) pays a visit to the camp, where Stan attempts to fix his leaking car radiator by filling it with rice. The radiator explodes, and everyone ends up in a rice fight.

Production: As soon as the Roach lot reopened in late August 1929, it was back to work for Laurel and Hardy and straight to prison for Stan and Ollie. The chain gang sequence was filmed at the Roach Ranch, near Arnaz Drive in Beverly Hills, and the opening prison sequence was shot in a real prison yard.

One of the hazards of making slapstick comedy is the possibility of injury, and Oliver Hardy's widow, Lucille, said he received just such an injury during the antics with the pick axes. However, it was worth it, with reviews like this one from *Motion Picture Magazine*: "Slapstick, pure and simple, but if you don't laugh yourself silly you must have lockjaw..."

Classic Dialogue: A new Hardy catchphrase, "Why don't you be careful" pops up twice here. "Come, Stanley" makes a first appearance.

L&H Moments: Ollie does his tie-fiddling business for the first time in the sound shorts, Ollie gives an extended look to the camera when he's hit in the face by some flying rice.

Verdict: This is a prime example of what by now had become pretty standard Laurel and Hardy fare. 3/5

The Rogue Song

Producer Irving G Thalberg (uncredited). Director Lionel Barrymore. Story Frances Marion & John Colton, based on *Gypsy Love* by Franz Lehar. Written & filmed July-September 1929. Laurel & Hardy signed 19 September 1929. Released 17 January 1930. 115 minutes. Two colour Technicolor. With Lawrence Tibbett, Catherine Dale Owen

Story: Yegor (Tibbett), a 'singing bandit,' and his two sidekicks, Ali-Bek (Laurel) and Muraz-Bek (Hardy), battle the Cossacks. Despite his hatred of Cossacks, Yegor falls in love with Cossack Princess Vera (Owen), whose brother is a Cossack commander.

Production: One of the 'lost' Laurel and Hardy films, no complete surviving copy of *The Rogue Song* exists. MGM's print was destroyed in a fire in their vault, while the Technicolor Corporation disposed of its 'check prints' and negatives after a film was released. All that is available is a complete soundtrack, a three-minute clip of the storm sequence featuring Laurel and Hardy, a trailer lacking a soundtrack and one reel (10 minutes) of non-Laurel and Hardy footage.

Lawrence Tibbett was the star of the Metropolitan Opera, and when he signed to MGM he was promised a big, prestige movie. *The Rogue Song* was it, but according to Hal Roach, the finished film was too sombre, so Laurel and Hardy were called in to shoot additional scenes. Roach claimed he wrote and directed the Laurel and Hardy sequences, based on an original script which later formed the basis of *Fra Diavolo*. Hal Roach certainly didn't waste ideas, gags or effort.

Tibbett was recalled from New York to shoot one scene with Laurel and Hardy in an attempt to integrate them into the film. According to his son, though, Laurel and Hardy were in the film from the start. The disjointed nature of their scenes seems to back Roach's version.

The film premiered at Graumann's Chinese Theatre on Hollywood Boulevard, and Laurel and Hardy as well as star Tibbett appeared in a live radio broadcast direct from the theatre. Reviews were mixed, with *Variety* in particular singling out Laurel and Hardy's scenes for criticism: "...the supposed laugh footage is awkward and deplorably weak."

Other than the gimmick of *Hollywood Revue Of 1929*, *The Rogue Song* was the first time that Laurel and Hardy were co-opted by a bigger studio to work in a non-Laurel and Hardy film. It should have been taken as an example of how such films don't work, as Fox and Laurel and Hardy would discover in the 1940s.

Verdict: Most Laurel and Hardy fans can get by without tracking this one down...

Night Owls

Director James Parrott. Two reels. Written & filmed October-November 1929. Released by MGM, January 1930. With Edgar Kennedy, Anders Randolph, James Finlayson

Story: Police Officer Kennedy is in trouble with the Police Chief: there's been a string of robberies on his patch and no arrests. Kennedy meets vagrants Stan and Ollie and makes a deal with them: in exchange for not arresting them for vagrancy, they will break into the Chief's house, so Kennedy can stage an arrest. Stan and Ollie make a racket breaking in, but it is Kennedy who gets arrested for the robberies.

Production: Drawn from a Stan Laurel Vaudeville sketch (*The Nutty Burglar*, 1914), *Night Owls* was the first of the Laurel and Hardy talkies to be remade in foreign languages for overseas territories. It was reshot in Italian (*Ladroni*) and in Spanish (*Ladrones*). Later films would be made in German and French as well. Once the film was finished in English, it was translated into the additional languages then each scene was shot in each language in turn with all the actors, including Laurel and Hardy, learning their dialogue phonetically. Some Italian and Spanish talent was featured in the films, but actors like James Finlayson and Edgar Kennedy proved irreplaceable, so had to learn their dialogue in each language. It was a tortuous process, but one which paid off with amazing popularity for Laurel and Hardy outside of the US. The care and attention taken on these foreign language versions might go some way to explaining the continuing popularity of the team some 70 years after they started making sound films.

Classic Dialogue: "Why don't you keep quiet," asks Ollie of his partner in crime.

L&H Moments: Stan cries and pokes Ollie in the eye with his finger. There's a trouser tearing resulting in a classic Ollie look to camera, which culminates in complete trouser removal and climaxes with Stan in a can!

Verdict: A mixed bag. 3/5

5. The Sound Shorts, 1930

Blotto

Director James Parrott. Three reels. Written & filmed December 1929-January 1930. Released by MGM, February 1930. With Anita Garvin, Tiny Sandford, Frank Holliday

Story: Stan's wife (Garvin) won't allow him out as she knows he's planning a night on the tiles with Mr Hardy. Ollie has reservations at a nightclub, but there's no alcohol due to Prohibition. Stan plans to take a bottle his wife has stashed away, but she overhears his phone call, so replaces the liquor with her own concoction of Tabasco sauce, cold tea and mustard. Despite this, Stan and Ollie get drunk on the mixture, only to face an encounter with Mrs Laurel and a shotgun.

Production: Blotto was the team's first three-reel comedy. Three-reelers were made when the laughs or the story demanded it, even though the Roach Studio made no more money from a 30-minute three-reeler than a 20-minute two-reeler. Each year's production quota was ordered in advance by cinema circuits at a set price per film, usually for two-reelers. This was one of the most expensive Laurel and Hardy shorts as 2000 extras were recruited for the nightclub scenes. A Stan and Ollie song at the nightclub location was scripted but cut from the film.

This film was given the phonetic foreign language treatment: it became *La Vida Nocturna* in Spanish with Linda Loredo as Mrs Laurel and *Une Nuit Extravagante* in French with Georgette Rhodes in the wife role. These extended European editions featured extra scenes in the nightclub sequence, including a belly dancer and a woman doing a comic dance with balloons. There's also a scene in which an elegant woman sits in a seat the boys have drenched in soda water.

Although James Parrott continued to be the solely credited director on films like this, Stan Laurel signed a new contract with Roach Studios during December 1929 which described his role in the creation of the Laurel and Hardy shorts as 'Actor, Director, Writer.'

L&H Moments: Stan scratches his head in confusion for the first time in what would become another trademark gesture. Debuting in this short is Stan's ear-wiggling, rarely deployed but always to great comic effect. The bizarre effect was achieved by running the camera at a slow frame rate (8 or 12 frames per second instead of 24) and pulling Stan's ears with strings attached behind. Ollie's sniff of the bottle and nod of confirmation to the camera (and so to the audience) when Mrs Laurel explains what was in the bottle is a masterpiece of comic understatement, the kind of thing only Hardy could carry off.

Verdict: Blotto showed that Laurel and Hardy could sustain their brand of comedy at a longer length, allowing them to explore their characters in more depth. The first step on a very productive road. 4/5

Brats

Director James Parrott. Two reels. Written & filmed January-February 1930. Released by MGM, March 1930.

Story: Stan and Ollie try to relax at home with friendly games of draughts and pool, but their mischievous sons (miniature versions of Stan and Ollie) cause havoc. After chasing an animated mouse with a shotgun, the kids go to bed, having left the bath water running. After being serenaded by Stan and Ollie, Oliver Jr. demands a glass of water. His father opens the bathroom door to a comic deluge.

Production: Only the second film to feature just Laurel and Hardy in the cast, albeit doubled up. Their wives are out for 'target practice' according to a title card cut from the preview print, while the action was supposed to be taking place at the Hardy residence, an explanatory fact missing from the film. There's a clue to who one of the wives may be: watch for Jean Harlow's portrait on the mantelpiece.

There are very few optical tricks in *Brats*: the illusion that Stan and Ollie are in the room with junior versions of themselves was mostly achieved through careful editing. There are only two double exposure shots. The sets were constructed at three times normal size to achieve the scenes featuring Stan and Ollie junior.

Debuting on this film (although it was later dubbed onto releases of earlier films) was the trademark Laurel and Hardy 'cuckoo song,' written by T Marvin Hatley. He worked on a radio station on the Roach lot and had written the tune as a time signal to be played each hour. Laurel heard it and decided it was the ideal opener to the Laurel and Hardy pictures. The rest is musical and comedy history. French, German and Spanish versions were made of *Brats*.

Classic Dialogue: "If you must make a noise, then make it quietly," is a classic nonsensical instruction from Stan to the children, while his "You can lead a horse to water but a pencil must be lead," remains an aphorism by which many people live their lives.

Verdict: An absolute classic. In this film, Stan Laurel was able to very cleverly comment on the characters of Stan and Ollie and their relationship in a way that very few of the other films allowed. Here, the childlike adults actually get to play children and it's brilliant. 5/5

Below Zero

Director James Parrott. Two reels. Written & filmed February 1930. Released by MGM, April 1930. With Tiny Sandford, Frank Holliday, Blanche Payson, Bobby Burns

Story: During the bitter cold winter of 1929, Stan and Ollie are trying to earn a living as buskers. The choice of a deaf school as a prime location is not ideal. A run-in with an unimpressed music lover leads to a snowball fight and the destruction of the boys' instruments. Their fortunes change when Stan finds a wallet loaded with cash. Saved by a policemen from a street thug, the boys offer to buy him lunch, only to realise when the bill comes that it is the cop's wallet they've got. They soon pay the price and end up back on the street, with Stan in a freezing rain barrel.

Production: Almost silent, with dialogue only important at the end, *Below Zero* was a simple film to produce and is definitely a throwback to the silent days. The Spanish version (*Tiembla y titubea*) is longer at three reels and features a scene in which the cop wins a cash award from his boss, explaining the money in his wallet, and there's further business with cops (including a hat-swapping scene) when the boys are busking.

Classic Dialogue: When as unimpressed householder discovers the boys make about 50 cents per street, they say, "There's a dollar, move down a couple of streets."

L&H Moments: The expanding wallet made of many pockets – all empty – is great, as is Stan's slow look between the photograph in the wallet and the cop at the table as realisation slowly dawns. The physical gag at the end, where Stan is bloated after drinking the barrel's contents is another of the Laurel and Hardy trademark physical effects.

Verdict: Memorable stuff, *Below Zero* is a favourite. It's simple and the comedy is firmly rooted in character and situation: a situation which reflected the reality of life in America after the Wall Street crash of 1929. Despite being comedians, it could be argued that many of Laurel and Hardy's shorts of the 1930s had a strong social conscience while being hilariously funny. 4/5

Hog Wild

Director James Parrott. Two reels. Written & filmed April 1930. Released by MGM, May 1930. With Fay Holderness, Dorothy Granger

Working Titles: Hay Wire, Aerial Antics (UK title)

Story: Ollie's wife forces him to install the radio antenna on the roof. Stan helps. After destroying the chimney and falling from the roof, they take an impromptu tour of the town with Ollie atop a ladder in the back of Stan's out-of-control car.

Production: In early April 1930, the Hal Roach crew rented a vacant property lot in Culver City and built a fake house for Laurel and Hardy to climb all over. This short saw the debut of T Marvin Hatley's distinctive background music which was to be used in many of the Laurel and Hardy shorts, becoming recognisable to viewers the world over. It was Laurel's firm belief that strong backing music added much to his pantomime brand of comedy. As well as playing the maid, Dorothy Granger can be seen (from behind) as the woman raising her skirt to cross a puddle, almost causing Stan to have a car accident.

Hog Wild was the final film in the 1929-1930 production season, a run which had brought Roach studios a profit of $140,000. As the nation fell into depression following the October 1929 Wall Street crash, so did the film business and Hal Roach Studios was to suffer financially over the next few years.

Verdict: The final run in the car is a riot, but the clambering about the rooftop is standard slapstick stuff which doesn't rely enough on the characters of Stan and Ollie to make this any more than average. 3/5

The Laurel-Hardy Murder Case

Director James Parrott. Three reels. Written & filmed May 1930. Released by MGM, September 1930. With Fred Kelsey, Del Henderson, Dorothy Granger, Frank Austin, Tiny Sandford

Working Titles: That's That, The Rap

Story: Fishing for their next meal, vagrants Stan and Ollie receive word that wealthy Ebeneezer Laurel has passed away. Figuring that Stan may be in line for a huge inheritance, the boys show up at the Laurel mansion on a dark and stormy night. They discover that old Ebeneezer has been murdered, and they (along with the other Laurel heirs) are considered suspects. They spend a terror-filled night in the mansion before awakening back on the fishing docks, their experience having been a dream.

Production: From the opening in which the credits are read aloud by twin girls in a proscenium arch through to the cop-out ending in which it's all a dream, this has to be the most bizarre Laurel and Hardy film made.

The film was originally supposed to be a straightforward murder mystery solved in the end by detective Fred Kelsey, who takes the credit from Stan and Ollie (who really solved the case) with the declaration "That's that!"

No less than three foreign versions of this short were made: *Feu Mon Oncle, Der Spuk Um Mitternacht* and *Noche Duendes* in French, German and Spanish. These foreign editions featured an extra reel of material in which Stan and Ollie travel to the Laurel Mansion by train. Most of the gags were reworked from *Berth Marks.*

Kelsey's exclamation of "That's that!" became the title of a gag reel put together in 1937 by film editor Bert Jordan as a gift for Stan Laurel. The footage consist mainly of out-takes, foreign language extracts and bloopers from *The Laurel-Hardy Murder Case* and *Way Out West.*

Just before shooting began Stan suffered a personal tragedy when his one-week-old son, Stanley Robert Jefferson, died. His wife Lois gave birth on 7 May 1930, two months prematurely. Stan's son only survived until 16 May 1930.

Classic Dialogue: "I'm gonna get half of everything that's coming to you," demands Ollie, not realising what he's letting himself in for. "Well, here's another nice mess you've gotten me into!" makes its debut in dialogue in this film.

Verdict: Pure classic, it's just a shame this turns out to be a dream, as we'd all love to see the resolution to the mystery, especially as Stan and Ollie are instrumental in uncovering the culprits. This three-reeler was another step on the way to feature films - the secondary characters get more screen time and Stan and Ollie are part of a larger story which doesn't revolve around them. 5/5

Another Fine Mess

Director James Parrott. Three reels. Written & filmed September-November 1930. Released by MGM, November 1930. With Thelma Todd, James Finlayson, Charles Gerrard

Story: Escaping a pursuing cop, Stan and Ollie hide out in the empty mansion of Colonel Buckshot. A couple arrive to rent the mansion, so Ollie poses as the owner, while Stan doubles as both butler and maid. The real Colonel Buckshot (Finlayson) returns home, only to call the cops on the 'burglars.' The boys escape, dressed as a water buffalo riding on a tandem bicycle.

Production: This is the debut of musician Le Roy Shield who was brought in to score the first Laurel and Hardy feature film *Pardon Us*, filming at the same time. He stayed around and scored many of the recurring background tunes which would turn up again and again in the sound shorts.

Classic Dialogue: It's hackneyed now, but the exchange "Call me a cab" and "You're a cab" is still very funny.

L&H Moments: "Well, here's another nice mess you've gotten me into" pops up, and is misquoted for the film's title.

Verdict: Based on a vaudeville sketch (*Home From the Honeymoon*, 1908) by Stan's father, *Another Fine Mess* shows its age. Some of the masquerade is fun, but it feels like Laurel and Hardy are resting on their Laurels (ahem!) here. 3/5

Be Big

Director James Parrott. Three reels. Written & filmed December 1930. Released by MGM, February 1931. With Anita Garvin, Isabelle Keith, Baldwin Cooke, Charlie Hall

Working Title: The Chiselers

Story: While Stan, Ollie, and their wives are preparing for an Atlantic City vacation, Stan and Ollie are invited to a stag party that evening. Ollie pretends to be ill and tells the girls that he and Stan will join them in Atlantic City the next morning. The boys don their lodge uniforms and spend most of the film wrestling with Ollie's feet stuck in Stan's too-tight boots.

Production: This was Anita Garvin's last Laurel and Hardy appearance until 1938. She devoted herself to bringing up her children, despite Laurel's repeated attempts to tempt her back. She was often replaced by Mae Busch.

Be Big was paired up with the extended three-reel version of *Laughing Gravy* and released as one-hour feature films in France and Spain under the titles *Les Carottiers* and *Les Calaveras*. Each film features subtle differences from the English language originals because of the reshoots. In particular, the foreign versions of *Be Big* feature even more of the boot business, including Ollie burning his backside on a radiator and almost falling out of the window, then getting his head caught up in an exercise machine. These sequences were not seen in the English language versions.

Classic Dialogue: "Don't stand there looking like a Sphinx" is Ollie's enigmatic instruction to Stan. Stan continues to muddle his aphorisms with "A cool head never won fair lady."

Verdict: This is the classic Laurel and Hardy situation: get rid of the wives for a night on the town, but it's not a classic film. It's not as funny as *Blotto* and the boots gag goes on too long. *Be Big* doesn't really justify its three-reel length and is a rare case of Laurel stretching his material a bit too thin. 2/5

6. The Sound Shorts, 1931

Chickens Come Home

Director James Horne. Three reels. Written & filmed December 1930-January 1931. Released by MGM, February 1931. With Mae Busch, Thelma Todd, James Finlayson, Norma Drew

Working Title: Sweeties

Story: Oliver Hardy is a manure merchant running for mayor. A gold-digging old flame (Mae Busch) appears on the scene and threatens to ruin both Ollie's ambitions and marriage (to Thelma Todd) unless he pays money to keep her quiet. He is hosting a lavish dinner party at his house that night, which she threatens to disrupt. Ollie sends Stan, his campaign manager, to her apartment to keep her at bay.

Production: A remake of 1927's *Love 'Em And Weep*, the addition of sound does little to raise this film above the original material. Here, though, Oliver Hardy is promoted to the businessman role and James Finlayson is a mere butler.

The economic downturn may have influenced the desire to do a straightforward remake. Roach Studios was suffering along with the rest of America through the 1930s and major players like Edgar Kennedy had their contracts terminated. Laurel and Hardy were big stars who were guaranteed work, but it would have to be done to a budget. For similar reasons only one foreign version of this was made: the Spanish *Politiquerias*. This features one of the few film appearances of magician Hadji Ali. He's a guest at Ollie's party (along with Mexican magician Abraham J Cantu).

Classic Dialogue: Ollie's idea of Mayoral speech writing: "And so forth, and so forth and so on." The classic catchphrase is shared as Ollie begins "Well..." and Stan completes: "Here's another fine mess I've gotten you into." Ollie's comment on Mrs Laurel's gullibility: "If she was dumb enough to marry you, she'll believe anything."

Verdict: It worked once, so why not twice! Didn't 1930s audiences notice that this was a remake of a film from three years before? These days they're called sequels. 3/5

The Stolen Jools

Producer Pat Casey. Director William McGann. Two reels. Produced early 1931. Released April 1931. Released in UK 1932 as *The Slippery Pearls.* With Buster Keaton, Our Gang, Joe E Brown, Edward G Robinson, Joan Crawford

Production: Bizarre short with an amazing cast, presented by National Variety Artists as a charity project to raise funds for the NVA tuberculosis sanatorium in New York, yet funded by the Chesterfield cigarette company! The irony obviously escaped everyone. Laurel and Hardy have one brief appearance, as sidekicks to detective Eddie Kane. They drive Kane in their standard Model-T Ford to the home of actress Norma Shearer, whose jewels ("jools") are missing.

Classic Dialogue: After the car collapses, Ollie tells Stan: "I told you not to make that last payment!"

Verdict: A brief bit part appearance, but the boys are at least true to type. 2/5

Laughing Gravy

Director James Horne. Two or three reels (two versions). Written & filmed February 1931. Released by MGM, April 1931. With Charlie Hall, Harry Bernard, Laughing Gravy

Story: In the middle of a bitter winter, Stan and Ollie are trying to hide a dog named Laughing Gravy from their landlord. The dog won't stop barking and the landlord (Hall) eventually throws his tenants out. However, his building has been quarantined. He walks off-camera to shoot himself (twice, if the soundtrack is to be believed).

Production: For over 50 years, American prints of this film existed only in two-reel form. In the mid-1980s, an English print was discovered of the long-lost third reel. The alternate ending sees Stan and Ollie packing to leave their apartment, just as Stan receives a telegram informing him that he is to receive a huge inheritance from a deceased uncle, but only if he cuts all ties with Ollie, whom his uncle felt was responsible for Stan's "deplorable" condition. Ollie is outraged that Stan won't share the contents of the telegram with him, but is understanding when he does read it. Stan decides to stay, but only so he won't have to leave his dog.

The switch to the newly-shot quarantine ending appears to have been a last-minute decision. Paperwork in the Roach files has the original plot crossed out and the notation 'new ending.'

The complete three-reel version of *Laughing Gravy* was cleverly added to Spanish and French versions of *Be Big* (entitled *Los Calaveras* and *Les Carottiers* respectively) as the events after Stan and Ollie's divorces from their wives. Each film is slightly different in detail as they were all reshot. Reshooting for foreign territories by Roach ended with *Laughing Gravy*. Despite the fact that revenues were good, the cost and effort were high and, in the depression of the 1930s, it was a luxury that couldn't be afforded, especially with the improvements in dubbing techniques.

The dog in *Laughing Gravy* turned up in *The Bohemian Girl* and the longer version of *Pardon Us*, as well as other Roach films of the time.

Verdict: An absolute classic: the perfect Laurel and Hardy short, at least in the two-reeler version. The three-reeler extends the film with no great benefit to the comedy and changes the tone of the whole piece. The comic despair of Hall as the landlord is both funny and cruel, but the best humour is. 5/5 for the two-reel version, 4/5 for the three-reel version. More is not necessarily better!

Our Wife

Director James Horne. Two reels. Written & filmed March 1931. Released by MGM, May 1931. With Jean 'Babe' London, James Finlayson, Ben Turpin, Charlie Rogers

Story: Ollie plans to marry his sweetheart Dulcie, but he's almost thwarted when Dulcie's father sees a picture of Ollie and forbids the marriage. The couple plan to elope. They manage to get away, despite Stan's 'help' and visit a Justice of the Peace. The cross-eyed justice (Turpin) accidentally marries Ollie to Stan.

Production: The longest scene in this short, as Stan, Ollie and Dulcie try to get into the tiny car Stan has rented, was based on just one line in the script: 'Go for ad lib business trying to get Babe [Oliver Hardy] and girl into the car.'

Classic Dialogue: "Goodbye" says Stan, forgetting that he's listening in to a private conversation. James Finlayson perfects his "D'oh" exclamation (later co-opted by Homer Simpson!)

L&H Moments: Stan's head-scratching begins to become a bit self-conscious and mannered from here onwards: a fate that would eventually befall all the Laurel and Hardy trademarks by the time of the poor feature films of the 1940s.

Verdict: After years of sharing the same bed, Stan and Ollie finally get married! Fin and Ben Turpin bring much needed sparkle to this elopement saga, while Stan suffers as the best man with little to do. Not one of the classics. 2/5

Come Clean

Director James Horne. Two reels. Written & filmed May 1931. Released by MGM, September 1931. With Mae Busch, Gertrude Astor, Linda Loredo, Charlie Hall, Eddie Baker, Tiny Sandford

Story: An evening alone awaits Mr and Mrs Hardy until Mr and Mrs Laurel pay a surprise visit. Stan develops a craving for ice cream, which means a trip to the soda fountain. On the way home, Stan and Ollie save a woman (Mae Busch) from an attempted suicide. Annoyed by their heroism, she insists they take her home and care for her. They try to escape, but she follows them. Stan and Ollie have to hide their unruly and unwelcome guest from their wives.

Production: The opening scene, where the Hardy couple hide from the Laurels, wasn't scripted, but improvised on set. It's basically a reworking by Laurel of the opening of *Should Married Men Go Home?* The blackmail storyline is lifted directly from *Chickens Come Home*, which was only released seven months previously.

Classic Dialogue: "Get my new hat," says Ollie, on his way to get ice cream. "You're going to get it in your hat?" queries Stan. Told there is no chocolate, Stan helpfully asks: "What other flavours are you out of?" and Charlie Hall provides a list. Ollie's wife gets to the basis of Stan and Ollie's characters: "Just because you've got the mind of a four-year-old, you don't have to display it."

Verdict: It's all here: the overbearing wives, the childish craving for ice cream, the inability to cope with the simple task of buying some, the sense of duty which sees Stan and Ollie go to the aid of Mae Busch, who then proceeds to play out her old blackmail routine. It's a classic. 4/5

One Good Turn

Director James Horne. Two reels. Written & filmed June 1931. Released by MGM, October 1931. With Mary Carr, James Finlayson, Billy Gilbert, Dorothy Granger, Snub Pollard

Story: Victims of the Depression, homeless Stan and Ollie are reduced to begging for food. A kindly old lady offers them a meal. As they dine, they overhear a conversation: the heartless landlord threatens to throw the old lady out of her home. Unaware that it's a play rehearsal, Stan and Ollie set out to raise money. They attempt to auction off their car, but Stan ends up the highest bidder. A drunk accidentally puts his wallet into Stan's pocket. Ollie finds it and thinks Stan has stolen the money from the old lady. When the truth is discovered, a vengeful Stan takes his revenge on Ollie.

Production: The original ending to *One Good Turn* saw the drunk (Billy Gilbert in his first film with Laurel and Hardy) from the car auction turn up to help the old woman keep her house. Seeing Stan and Ollie with his wallet, he declares them to be thieves and chases them off. The new ending, in which after years of abuse and torment Stan finally turns on Ollie, was partly inspired by Laurel's daughter. Lois declared herself scared of "Uncle Babe," Ollie, as he was always hitting her daddy. Laurel figured out a way to show he could get his own back...

The 1930-31 season of Laurel and Hardy films showed a loss in excess of $25,000, despite their ever-growing popularity. To continue financing the films, Roach agreed a loan of $75,000 from the Bank of America, offering up all rights to the first Laurel and Hardy feature film *Pardon Us* as collateral.

Classic Dialogue: Begging for food, Ollie says they haven't eaten for three days. Stan explains: "Yesterday, today and tomorrow."

L&H Moments: The whole camping sequence is great, from Stan slurping the soup to Ollie trying it for himself. Ollie's confused look as Stan gets small cups of water, unaware that the tent is burning.

Verdict: This short gets to the heart of the characters of Stan and Ollie: down on their luck constantly, but always out to help others no matter how low their own circumstances (even if they are wildly misguided). 4/5

Beau Hunks

Director James Horne. Four reels. Written & filmed July-August 1931. Released by MGM, December 1931. With Charles Middleton, Broderick O'Farrell, Harry Schultz, Abdul Kasim K'Horne (James Horne)

Story: To forget a woman, Ollie makes Stan join the French Foreign Legion with him. They discover that virtually every soldier has been jilted by the same woman (Jean Harlow). Ollie decides to quit the legion, but discovers it's not that easy. After a torturous march in the scorching desert sun, Stan and Ollie succeed in defending a nearby camp against an attack from the dreaded Riffs.

Production: Beau Hunks is the only Laurel and Hardy four-reeler, a non-standard length of 35 minutes. It was intended as a two-reeler, but kept getting longer as more gags were added during filming. Even though Roach Studios were set to lose money on the film (as it had been pre-sold to distributors at two-reel prices), it was felt that the quality of the film would suffer with editing, so it was extended.

The whole sequence at Fort Arid leading up to the arrival of reinforcements in the form of Stan and Ollie, appears to have been ad libbed during shooting because none of it was scripted. A scene in which Ollie plants dynamite among the Riffs and Stan accidentally sets it off was scripted but not shot. The climax was scripted very simply as 'A battle ensues, winding up with the Legion victorious.' It was up to Laurel, while shooting on the fort set, to come up with the solution: tacks on the Riffs' bare feet. The pay-off where the leader of the Riffs is shown to also have a photo of Jean Harlow was made up on the spot too! Thank goodness for creative inspiration.

Roach managed to get Jean Harlow for free. The actress who'd started at Roach before going to MGM, gave producer Hal Roach permission to use her photo for the 'everyone is in the Foreign Legion because of Jean Harlow' gag. The photo is from the Laurel and Hardy production *Double Whoopee*.

Legionnaire Louis Van DeNecker was a technical consultant. As well as making sure the rifles were handled appropriately, he took on the training of the would-be troops, including Stan and Ollie. Resident set doctors had to treat Laurel and Hardy for sunburn, while other extras suffered various cuts, bruises and eye injuries, all in the pursuit of laughs.

Director James Horne couldn't find an actor he liked for the leader of the Riffs, so he promptly rechristened himself Abdul Kasim K'Horne and took the role. This was the first of several appearances by Charles Middleton in Laurel and Hardy films – he is better known as galactic villain Ming the Merciless in the 1930s *Flash Gordon* serials. *Beau Hunks*, a vague parody of *Beau Geste*, was issued in Britain under the title *Beau Chumps*.

Classic Dialogue: Ollie announces he's to marry and Stan replies: "You don't believe me!" Asked who he's marrying, Ollie answers: "Why, a woman of course!" Stan is confused again: "There's someone knocking on the phone..."

Charles Middleton gets a great line, in response to Stan: "You forgot what you came here to forget? Well, I'll see you don't forget what you're here for!"

L&H Moments: Ollie announces his name as Oliver Norvell Hardy for the first time.

Verdict: Beau Hunks is crying out to be a feature film. It does almost everything right, lacking those musical longueurs or unfunny padding which some of the later Laurel and Hardy feature films suffer from. A film to be celebrated. 5/5

Any Old Port

Director James Horne. Two reels. Written & filmed September-November 1931. Released by MGM, March 1932. With Walter Long, Jacqueline Wells, Harry Bernard, Charlie Hall, Bobby Burns

Story: Stan and Ollie are sailors on leave who check into a cheap hotel. The hotel's owner, Mugsie Long, has trapped his innocent cleaning girl into marrying him. The boys help her escape, and Mugsie vows revenge. An old friend of Ollie's offers him some quick money if he'll fight in a boxing match. Ollie volunteers Stan for the task, and his opponent turns out to be Mugsie. Stan wins the fight when he puts on Mugsie's loaded glove, only to discover that Ollie has bet all their money on Mugsie!

Production: Why are Stan and Ollie sailors at the start of this short? An entirely different opening reel was shot (at San Pedro Harbour), which showed life aboard ship for sailors Stan and Ollie, their pet ostrich and Captain James Finlayson. After previews, the entire first reel was scrapped (losing Finlayson and Tiny Sandford from the film), the original second reel became the first reel, and a new ten-minute ending was shot – an example of the luxuries afforded Laurel and Hardy at the Roach Studio until new finance chief Henry Ginsberg got to grips with the cash flow.

The replacement material gives more coherence to the fight and much more comedic material for Stan Laurel to get his teeth into. Shot in Culver City Stadium, the boxing sequence boasted over 500 extras filling out the stadium seating to watch Battling Laurel in action.

Classic Dialogue: "We'd like a room with a Southern explosion," explains Stan. Walter Long on the phone: "I'm gonna be married! [Pause] Sure, she's conscious!" Ollie looks to the camera after Stan declares things to be "a terrible cats after me" instead of 'catastrophe.'

Verdict: I've got a soft spot for the boxing routine in *Any Old Port*, a vast improvement on *The Battle Of The Century*. Again, character is to the fore, but this short, like *Helpmates*, is simply not as great as the others from 1931. 3/5

On The Loose

Director Hal Roach. Two reels. Written & filmed October 1930. Released by MGM, 26 December 1931. With ZaSu Pitts, Thelma Todd, Claud Allister, John Loder, William (Billy) Gilbert, Charlie Hall

Story: Fed up with their boyfriends taking them to Coney Island, ZaSu and Thelma hope for more from an English gentleman who splashes their clothes with mud, but offers to buy them new outfits. After a trip to camp Billy Gilbert's women's outfitters, the girls are surprised by... another trip to Coney Island. Back home, the pair have unexpected new suitors: Stan and Ollie, also intent on a trip to... you guessed it!

Production: A Laurel and Hardy guest appearances in another Roach film. With Billy Gilbert, Charlie Hall and all the familiar musical themes in places, this feels like a Laurel and Hardy film without Laurel and Hardy.

Classic Dialogue: None to speak of.

Verdict: Nothing more than a punchline, using Laurel and Hardy as the joke, and no on-screen credit preserves the surprise. This probably went down well at the time, but *On The Loose* is far from a Laurel and Hardy film. A curiosity. 1/5

Helpmates

Director James Parrott. Two reels. Written & filmed October 1931. Released by MGM, January 1932. With Blanche Payson, Robert Callahan, Bobby Burns

Story: Ollie's wife is on a trip, so he has enjoyed a wild party. With her due back at noon, he enlists Stan to help tidy up. Not a good idea as he ruins two of Ollie's suits, destroys his kitchen and, finally, burns down his house entirely. *Helpmates* ends with Ollie, alone in his charred frame of a house, sitting in his chair in the rain.

Production: With the arrival of Henry Ginsberg to control the Roach Studio finances, for the first time Laurel faced a challenge to his control of the films. Ginsberg felt they could be produced faster and cheaper.

Classic Dialogue: "I was here, with me," explains Stan, unhelpful as ever. Comparing himself to Cinderella after doing all the cleaning up, Stan says to Ollie, "If I had any sense I'd walk out on you." "It's a good thing you don't," says Ollie. "It certainly is," agrees Stan, who then spends some time trying to figure out what's wrong with that conversation.

L&H Moments: There's Ollie's ostentatious signature and the first of Stan's confused explanations about what happens when "the mice are away." The way Stan opens the door rather then step through the frame is a lovely touch, while we know his attempt to light a fire with a match, then kerosene, is leading to trouble. He tearfully explains what happened to Ollie: "The house burnt down and I couldn't help it!"

Verdict: This would have been a classic in almost any other year, but it pales slightly in comparison to the almost perfect Laurel and Hardy films of 1931. 3/5

7. The Sound Shorts, 1932

The Music Box

Director James Parrott. Three reels. Written & filmed December 1931. Released by MGM, April 1932. With Billy Gilbert, Lilyan Irene, Sam Lufkin, Charlie Hall

Story: The simple job of delivering a piano to a house atop an enormous flight of stairs proves to be a trial for Stan and Ollie. Their attempts to carry the piano up the stairs result in it crashing into the street below four times, often with Ollie in tow. They finally succeed in getting the piano in the house, where they manage to wreck the living room. The owner of the house, Professor Theodore Von Schwarzenhoffen, returns and is outraged at the sight. He attacks the piano with an axe, but regrets his actions when he discovers it was a present from his wife.

Production: It's the one-gag Laurel and Hardy film, succinctly encapsulated as 'The boys try to deliver a piano.' Of course, *The Music Box* is a partial remake of *Hats Off*, and even returns to the flight of steps featured in the earlier film between 923 and 937 Vendome Street in the Silver Lake District of LA. According to Billy Gilbert he was originally set to direct the film, but instead took the role of blustering Professor Theodore Von Schwarzenhoffen.

There was a real piano inside the packing case. Stan Laurel felt it was necessary to convey the correct weight. The piano hacked to pieces at the climax was a fake made of balsa wood and bits from other pianos which had been demolished around the Roach lot.

The Music Box was the only Laurel and Hardy film to get an Academy Award, for Best Short Subject Comedy (1931-32). The award was presented on 18 November 1932 at The Ambassador Hotel, Cocoanut Grove. The film was also Laurel's personal favourite of the 106 Laurel and Hardy shorts and features.

L&H Moments: The boys appear in their working-men dungarees outfits. The moment where Ollie exchanges glances with the horse the second time he prepares to lower the piano on his back is priceless. *The Music Box* contains one of the best examples of the classic Laurel and Hardy swapped-hats routine, as it is cleverly sustained and built upon. The tidying-up of the house routine to the piano's patriotic songs is positively inspired.

Verdict: Laurel and Hardy's only Oscar winner, *The Music Box* is rightly hailed as an all-time great. 5/5

The Chimp

Director James Parrott. Three reels. Written & filmed January, 1932. Released by MGM, May 1932. With Billy Gilbert, James Finlayson, Charles Gemora, Tiny Sandford

Working Title: Monkeydoodle

Story: Stan and Ollie work in a run-down circus, which has more people in the ring than in the audience. The circus closes, and the owner divides its assets among the company. Instead of payment, Stan gets the flea circus, while Ollie gets the considerably larger Ethel the gorilla. They take the chimp back to their boarding house and attempt to hide it from their landlord.

Production: The circus scenes were shot in a genuine circus tent, rented and erected on the Roach ranch near Arnaz Drive, Beverly Hills. Stan Laurel's daughter, Lois, is in the audience. Ethel, the human chimpanzee, was played by Charles Gemora, a Philippine-born make-up artist and part-time gorilla impersonator (which career brought in the most money?). He returned to monkey around in *Swiss Miss*.

Classic Dialogue: "You look better in that end than I do," says Stan to Ollie, trying to convince him that he should remain as the back end of the pantomime horse.

L&H Moments: The sight of Ollie dressed as Ethel and Ethel in Ollie's clothes has to be seen to be believed! Ollie's delicate sprinkling of gunpowder into the circus canon is so fastidious, it's like he's adding seasoning to a favourite recipe.

Verdict: The Chimp looks like a feature-film scenario which doesn't even live up to its potential as a short. The opening circus scenes are calling out to be expanded, but the second half is yet another remake of *Angora Love* or *Laughing Gravy*, and a lazy one at that. 3/5

County Hospital

Director James Parrott. Two reels. Written & filmed February 1932. Released by MGM, June 1932. With Billy Gilbert, William Austin, May Wallace

Working Title: Forty Winks

Story: A visit from Stan to Ollie in hospital leads to both men being thrown out, despite Ollie's broken leg. Before leaving, Stan sits on a hypodermic needle filled with sedative. Driving Ollie home, he nearly falls asleep at the wheel, and the car careens wildly through the streets.

Production: 1930s cost-cutting at the Laurel and Hardy production unit finally started to affect the quality of the films from *County Hospital* onwards. Denied the funds to create the elaborate sequence in which a doped-up Stan drives his Model-T through town and encounters some business with a fire water hydrant and a steamroller, the team resorted to using very poor back-projection.

56

This was nowhere near as convincing as some of their stunts of the past and lets the film down badly.

During a tour of South America, as *County Hospital* was being made, Hal Roach announced that Laurel and Hardy would soon be seen in two feature-length films, starting with *Pack Up Your Troubles*.

L&H Moments: Stan eating a boiled egg – and the fact that he'd brought his own salt with him – is a nice character moment.

Verdict: It's interesting in this film to see Stan on his own in the world without Ollie, and the material in the hospital is fun (given their usual problems, it's a wonder one or the other wasn't in hospital before now). However, *County Hospital* is let down badly by the dire back-projection. 2/5

Scram!

Director Raymond McCarey. Two reels. Written & filmed June-July 1932. Released by MGM, September 1932. With Vivien Oakland, Rychard Cramer, Arthur Housman

Story: Arrested for vagrancy and told to leave town by the judge, Stan and Ollie encounter a good-natured drunk. They help him retrieve his lost keys, so he invites them to spend the night at his place. The drunk leads them to the wrong house, where Stan and Ollie help themselves to some silk pyjamas and get blotto with the lady of the house. The real owner returns home and it is, of course, the judge, who told the boys to "scram" in the first place.

Production: A rushed production due to impending vacation time for Stan Laurel, *Scram* packed a lot of simple but very funny business into its two reels. Material was lifted from *Night Owls* (breaking into the house) and improved upon. Arthur Housman would return to Laurel and Hardy films with his drunk act in *The Live Ghost, The Fixer-Uppers, Our Relations* and (very briefly) *The Flying Deuces*.

The 1932 trip Laurel took to Britain, accompanied by Oliver Hardy who fancied trying the golf courses, was intended as a holiday during the Roach Studios annual shutdown, but such was their amazing appeal to audiences that they were mobbed at every port and railway station en route. A door was torn from their car by a 2,000-strong crowd who turned out for their personal appearance at Leicester Square. Nine people were hospitalised out of a 6,000-strong crowd that greeted the boys at Glasgow's Central Station and Central Hotel. A visit to Paris drew further crowds, causing the team to cancel their hoped-for touring holiday of Europe. Returning to Los Angeles in mid-September 1932, Laurel and Hardy had discovered they were movie stars.

L&H Moments: The helpfulness of Stan and Ollie as they try to get back Housman's keys, despite the rain and their own predicament, really gets to the heart of their characters. Stan searching Ollie's pockets is a sign of their easy intimacy. Their living it up as guests and infectious laughter, not to mention the risqué drunken wrestling with the lady of the house all draw on their innocent, childlike characters.

Verdict: A classic situation comedy, *Scram!* features lots of good business and some great character moments for Laurel and Hardy. 3/5

Their First Mistake

Director George Marshall. Two reels. Written & filmed September 1932. Released by MGM, November 1932. With Mae Busch, Billy Gilbert, George Marshall

Story: Mrs Hardy has finally had it with her husband devoting more attention to Stan than to her. To escape her anger, Ollie locks himself away in Stan's apartment. Stan convinces Ollie to adopt a baby in order to save his marriage. When they return home with the infant, Ollie receives word that his wife is suing him for divorce. Stan and Ollie now have a baby to look after.

Production: Director George Marshall appears here as a neighbour congratulating Stan and Ollie on their new baby (he was also in *Pack Up Your Troubles*). A sequence was shot and then cut of Mrs Hardy getting advice from her parents that a baby would help save the marriage. The original gag ending had her returning to the Hardy household with newly adopted twins, resulting in three babies to look after!

Classic Dialogue: "I'm not as dumb as you look," claims Stan, while Ollie replies "You bet your life you're not!" Asked why he lit a match to look at the light switch in the dark, Stan explains: "I wanted to see if the switch was off."

Verdict: Despite having no resolution and being somewhat close to the bone in some areas (dealing with collapsing marriages and unwanted children) *Their First Mistake* is still a funny film, with all the best material drawn from the Stan and Ollie characters. It's especially strong on dialogue. 4/5

Towed In A Hole

Director George Marshall. Two reels. Written & filmed October-November 1932. Released December 1932. With Billy Gilbert

Working Title: Live Bait

Story: Fishmongers Stan and Ollie decide to buy a boat so they can catch their own fish, eliminate the middleman and have the profits go to the fish. They buy a run-down old boat, and have some fun repairing and painting it.

Production: Based on an early, unused outline for a film entitled *Live Bait*, *Towed In A Hole* dumped the dinner party opening and fish-catching gags in the outline and moved straight to the restoration of a boat, resulting in a 20-minute classic. The idea came from director George Marshall, who saw a fish-selling van on the streets of Culver City and decided something similar would be the ideal vehicle for Stan and Ollie.

The script/outline was very short, with comedy business all worked out during the shooting. The original ending of the film, where the boat sails off into the streets of Culver City causing havoc, was never filmed, partly due to the fact that two reels of material had been shot just rebuilding the boat, but also due to cost-cutting at Hal Roach Studios. In fact, studio manager Henry Ginsberg's cost-cutting led to the departure of director George Marshall from the Roach lot after this film.

Classic Dialogue: Stan attempts to explain his plan a second time: "If you caught a fish, whoever you sold it to, you wouldn't have to pay for it and the profits would go to the fish." Ollie replies with: "I know exactly what you mean." Ollie gets to the heart of the appeal of Laurel and Hardy: "Here we are, two grown-up men acting like a couple of children."

L&H Moments: Stan plays himself at tick-tack-toe by looking away when he takes a turn against himself.

Verdict: Absolutely top-notch Laurel and Hardy, *Towed In A Hole* is a near-perfect example of their short films. As with *Their First Mistake*, it's the depth of character and the increasingly surreal dialogue which make this a hit. 5/5

Twice Two

Director James Parrott. Two reels. Written & filmed December 1932. Released by MGM, February 1933. With Baldwin Cooke, Charlie Hall

Story: Stan and Ollie are themselves, as well as each other's wife. The two couples plan a lavish dinner party to celebrate their mutual anniversaries, but the wives prove just as inept as their husbands in dealing with things such as food and utensils.

Production: Stan Laurel's own real-life separation from his wife Lois may have been behind this comedy of marital disharmony which draws on the clever duplication device of *Brats*. Stan and Ollie's female voices were dubbed by Carol Tevis and May Wallace.

This was James Parrott's last Laurel and Hardy film.

Classic Dialogue: "She told me not to tell you there's a surprise," admits Stan, innocently. "So don't tell me," replies Ollie. "I won't. I can keep a secret," says Stan. Ollie tells Stan: "Why, you've forgotten more than he'll ever know."

Verdict: With Ollie in drag for the first time, and Laurel and Hardy married to each other, it's easy to see why *Twice Two* is a memorable short. It's worth it for Stan's attempt to buy ice cream alone. 4/5

8. The Sound Shorts, 1933

Me And My Pal

Directors Charles Rogers & Lloyd French. Two reels. Written & filmed March 1933. Released by MGM, April 1933. With James Finlayson, Eddie Dunn, Bobby Dunn, Frank Terry, James C Morton

Working Title: The Best Man

Story: Arriving at the Hardy home just before Ollie's society wedding, Stan's gift of a jigsaw puzzle proves extremely diverting; so much so that before long, Stan, Ollie, the butler, a cab driver, a cop and a delivery boy get caught up in completing it. Ollie misses his wedding, much to the annoyance of the bride's father (Finlayson).

Production: For the only time on a Laurel and Hardy short, two directors were credited on screen. French had been assistant director on most of the team's shorts since 1927 and had just signed a two-year contract with Roach as a writer/director.

The finale of *Me And My Pal* was never fully developed as the whole film was rushed through production due to overruns on *Fra Diavolo*. Laurel was still editing that feature film while he was making this short to maintain the Roach Studios release schedule. Just after this short was released, Stan's wife Lois filed for divorce which, according to Hal Roach, seriously affected Laurel's later career: "After that, Stan married all those other dames and it cost him a lot of money."

Classic Dialogue: "You know what a magnate is, don't you?" asks Ollie, to be greeted with the reply from Stan: "Sure, a thing that eats cheese." James Finlayson has a classic line: "What are you trying to do? Make me out to be a bigger fool than I look,... er, than I am!"

Verdict: An absolute triumph! *Me And My Pal* is the quintessential Laurel and Hardy sound short, taking a simple idea - the addictive, distracting nature of the jigsaw - and bringing Stan and Ollie's established characters into play. Taking a single element to absurd, but uncannily logical, extremes is the key to all great comedy and that's what *Me And My Pal* is: a truly great film comedy. 5/5

The Midnight Patrol

Director Lloyd French. Two reels. Written & filmed June-July 1933. Released by MGM, August 1933. With Frank Terry, Frank Brownlee, Eddie Dunn

Working Title: Calling All Cars

Story: Novice cops Stan and Ollie encounter a safe-breaker, whom they tell off. They then investigate a report of a home intruder and destroy the house before discovering that it is the home of their police chief, who had locked himself out.

Production: This last comedy of the 1932-33 season could not have come soon enough for Stan Laurel and Oliver Hardy. Just one month after Lois Laurel filed for divorce, Oliver Hardy made moves to divorce his wife Myrtle, blaming her alcoholism for breakdowns in the marriage in 1929 and 1931. These problems in the boys' private lives, however, didn't seem to be affecting their on-screen comedy.

Classic Dialogue: After Stan inadvertently writes an address across two sheets of paper, he says: "I wrote it on here and somebody's stolen the street!"

L&H Moments: Stan and Ollie compare diaries with the safe-breaker to find a convenient court date.

Verdict: Laurel and Hardy as cops is asking for trouble. Clearly the criminal element doesn't take them seriously – and no wonder. Not quite as funny as it could have been, this is a riff on *Scram!*, with the house turning out to be that of the Police Chief. 3/5

Busy Bodies

Director Lloyd French. Two reels. Written & filmed July 1933. Released by MGM, October 1933. With Charlie Hall, Tiny Sandford

Story: Stan and Ollie work at a lumber yard, which provides plenty of opportunity for chaos with tools, paint, nails and electric saws.

Production: Much of the business in *Busy Bodies* was concocted on set, as most of it doesn't appear in the written scenario, including the business with the plank, the pipe in the wall and the window frame. The characters played by Charlie Hall and Tiny Sandford don't appear in the initial scenario either. Often, Stan Laurel would develop his best funny business while messing about in front of the camera and seeing comic possibilities in the set which weren't evident when drafting the scenario. The car gag at the climax was a special effect, with each half running through separately, then composited on an optical printer. This was done for safety reasons, as even Laurel and Hardy weren't daft enough to tangle with a bandsaw.

L&H Moments: Stan pulls Ollie around by the brush glued to his chin.

Verdict: The ideal setting for chaos, Laurel and Hardy take every opportunity to break something or inflict injury... all to raise a laugh. 3/5

Wild Posies

Producer Robert F McGowan for Hal Roach. Director Robert F McGowan. Two reels. Written & filmed August 1933. Released October 1933. With Our Gang, Franklin Pangborn, Emerson Treacy, Gay Seabrook

Story: Spanky and family try hard to have a family photo taken, but fall foul of fussy photographer Otto Phocus.

Production: Another of Laurel and Hardy's minor cameo appearances: the boys appear in a gag as "the two most photogenic children" a photographer has ever seen. The huge chair from *Brats* is used to make Stan look child-sized.

Verdict: Well, it is only a 20-second appearance: for completists only. However, no print of the film is available at the time of writing. 1/5

Dirty Work

Director Lloyd French. Two reels. Written & filmed July-August 1933. Released by MGM, November 1933. With Lucien Littlefield, Sam Adams, Jiggs the Chimp

Story: Stan and Ollie are chimney sweeps who set out to clean mad scientist Professor Noodle's chimney. Noodle has discovered the secret to eternal youth and decided the two guys wrecking his house might be ideal test subjects. Stan accidentally knocks Ollie into a vat of the rejuvenating liquid. He's rejuvenated as a monkey with a derby, who mutters Ollie's phrase: "I have nothing to say."

Production: The personal lives of Laurel and Hardy had taken a turn for the better, with both men reconciled with their respective wives, Lois and Myrtle. It wasn't to be a state of affairs that would last long.

Classic Dialogue: The butler feels the chimney sweeps are less than adequate: "Somewhere an electric chair is waiting." "He went somewhere to look for an electric chair," says Stan of the butler.

L&H Moments: Ollie, sitting in the fireplace, is hit by six falling bricks, one after another.

Verdict: Habeas Corpus meets *Hog Wild.* The final gag is worth waiting for and Sam Adams makes a wonderfully sardonic butler, but it's not a classic. 3/5

Hollywood Party

Producers Harry Rapf & Howard Deitz. No director credit. 68 Minutes. Written & filmed March 1933-March 1934. Released June 1934. With Jimmy Durante, Lupe Velez, Charles Butterworth, Tom Kennedy, Eddie Quillan

Story: Durante, a former jungle picture star, wants to reclaim his lost glory by wrestling a pair of lions he's buying from Baron Munchausen. Stan and Ollie turn up at a party at Munchausen's home to return his worthless cheque and reclaim their lions. They end up in a tit-for-tat egg battle with Mexican actress Lupe Velez, before releasing the lions to terrorise the party-goers.

Production: An all-star Hollywood film with a troubled production history, *Hollywood Party* nonetheless features an extended Laurel and Hardy cameo. Various stars were attached to the project, but over time many dropped out. Laurel and Hardy worked on their scenes from 21 September, under the guidance of their old cameraman George Stevens, improvising the egg sequence with Lupe Velez (reused by Laurel in *The Bullfighters*). They spent four days on the project before returning to pre-production on *Sons Of The Desert*. When the film was released, Laurel and Hardy won accolades from *The Hollywood Reporter*: "One of the funniest sequences to be seen in pictures. It had preview audiences rolling in the aisles. The sequence is worth the price of admission..."

L&H Moments: Stan looks in Ollie's pocket and his expression confirms that there is a smashed egg in there; Ollie gives a priceless look to camera as a egg goes down his trousers.

Verdict: This actually works quite well on its own, divorced from the rest of the film. A bit more work and structure and it could have made a stand-alone Laurel and Hardy short. 2/5

Oliver The Eighth

Director Lloyd French. Three reels. Written & filmed December 1933-January 1934. Released by MGM, February 1934. With Mae Busch, Jack Barty

Working Title: The Private Life of Oliver The Eighth

Story: Stan and Ollie are barbers who both answer a personal ad from a wealthy widow. The widow has murdered seven husbands, each named Oliver, making Ollie her eighth victim. The boys spend a terror-filled night in the widow's mansion, coping with her and the weird butler. As the knife is about to cut Ollie's throat, he awakens in a barber chair to find Stan shaving him; it was all a dream.

Production: During production, Laurel's 33-year-old brother Everett, known as Teddy, died of heart failure after receiving an anaesthetic at a dentist.

Classic Dialogue: Stan gets to deliver one of his mangled explanations: "If beauty was only skin deep, I would take some of the money and have her skinned, then she'd be able to look at a clock without having to work hard anymore, then I could scrape her chin if I didn't have to work hard anymore." After Stan shoots a hole in Ollie's long johns, he points out that "It was a good thing you weren't inside them!" Stan gets confused: "I was dreaming I was awake and then I woke up to find myself asleep!" Ollie complains of his treatment: "Isn't it bad enough that I'm going to get my throat cut, without you trying to shoot me first?"

Verdict: Great until the 'it was all a dream' cop out, lifted direct from *The Laurel-Hardy Murder Case.* 3/5

9. The Sound Shorts, 1934-35

Going Bye-Bye

Director Charles Rogers. Two reels. Written & filmed May 1934. Released by MGM, June 1934. With Walter Long, Mae Busch, Harry Dunkinson, Sam Lufkin

Working Titles: Public Enemies, On Their Way Out

Story: Stan and Ollie are key witnesses in a trial that sends criminal Butch Long to jail for life. Butch swears revenge on the boys. They plan to leave town, and advertise in the paper for a travelling companion. The woman who responds to their ad turns out to be Butch's girlfriend. Butch accidentally locks himself in a trunk; Stan and Ollie, not knowing who is inside, try to free him with blow torches and hoses. Once free, Butch carries out his threat to break their legs and tie them around their heads.

Production: After the production delays on *Babes In Toyland*, the final two shorts due for the 1933-34 production cycle were made in a hurry. This one drew on the then-current manhunt for 'public enemy number one' John Dillinger.

The big finishes to many of these shorts were not scripted. In the scenario for *Going Bye-Bye*, the gag sheet simply reads: 'We go for a wow finish and fade out.' It was up to Stan Laurel to turn that into a great send-off gag.

Classic Dialogue: With no petrol for their car Stan asks: "What are we gonna run it on," only to receive the answer, "the road," from Ollie. This film includes the all-time classic line from Ollie (on the phone to Mae Busch): "Excuse me, please, my ear is full of milk." Mae Busch's explanation for her friend getting locked in the trunk: "He was packing and he accidentally fell in." Stan and Ollie look at one another for a moment before Stan says: "It could happen."

Verdict: Absolute classic of the form. Stan and Ollie's self-awareness reveals they know they live in an absurd world. This is also the first time the "Well, here's another nice mess" line is used as a climatic punchline. The perfect Laurel and Hardy short and the start of a run of greats. 5/5

Them Thar Hills

Director Charles Rogers. Two reels. Written & filmed May-June 1934. Released by MGM, July 1934. With Charlie Hall, Mae Busch, Billy Gilbert

Story: Stan and Ollie are in the mountains so that Ollie can get the rest and relaxation he needs to cure his gout-stricken foot. They park their camping trailer next to a well filled with the discarded product of local moonshiners. They are visited by a couple who need gas for their car. The husband returns to the car, while the wife stays behind with Stan and Ollie; the three of them get blotto on the 'water' from the well. The husband returns, outraged, and a full-scale war develops.

Production: Much of this film was improvised on the spot within the broad scenario of a camping trip, giving the whole thing a very natural spontaneity. Scheduled to be shot in six days, filming dragged on for nine, due to heavy fog on location in the Santa Ynez Canyon. The entire outdoor setting for the film had to be duplicated (at great expense) on the Hal Roach soundstages.

Classic Dialogue: According to Stan, the boys will camp "right up in the high multitudes." He's also sure of the beneficial effects: "One month up here and we wouldn't know each other!"

Verdict: Fantastic stuff: Charlie Hall finally takes centre stage and, boy, does he deserve it (and everything that happens to him). This is a classic of the tit-for-tat school of comedy and led to a direct sequel under that very title. 5/5

The Live Ghost

Director Charles Rogers. Two reels. Written & filmed October-November 1934. Released by MGM, December 1934. With Walter Long, Arthur Housman, Mae Busch, Charlie Hall

Story: A gruff sea captain enlists Stan and Ollie to help him shanghai a crew for his next voyage. They succeed, but are also shanghaied aboard a "ghost ship." When a drunken crewmember is caked in whitewash, Stan and Ollie are convinced they've seen a ghost and try to dispose of the body.

Production: In the original opening to this Stan and Ollie were not merely fishing on the dock, but were in fact there to commit suicide (an idea revived in *The Flying Deuces*) before being persuaded by Captain Long to help recruit sailors for his ship. The entire production was shot in just one week.

Classic Dialogue: "I heard the ocean is infatuated with sharks," claims Stan. "Infuriated," corrects Ollie. "Do you have to take your own coal with you when you go to the other place," asks Stan of Hell.

L&H Moments: Ollie rips their first dollar in half to stop either one spending it.

Verdict: A very atmospheric and funny short, *The Live Ghost* only pales as it is surrounded by such high-calibre funnies. 4/5

Tit For Tat

Director Charles Rogers. Two reels. Written & filmed December 1934. Released by MGM, January 1935. With Charlie Hall, Mae Busch, James C Morton, Bobby Dunn

Story: Stan and Ollie own a new electrical supply store. Their neighbours are the Halls, owners of Hall's Grocery Store, the same couple Stan and Ollie encountered during their camping trip (*Them Thar Hills*). Mr Hall is not in a mood to forgive and forget, and another full-scale war develops, leaving both stores wrecked.

Production: The only Laurel and Hardy sequel. *Them Thar Hills* was such a success a rematch with Mr Hall was put into production. Most of the slapstick was suggested by props on the set, and Laurel and Hardy largely ignored many of the scripted gags or stunts and developed their own routines on the sound stage. As budgets were being reduced at Roach, the Culver City location shooting of a few years before was a thing of the past. Hence, the street for *Tit For Tat* was created entirely in the studio, which also allowed a greater degree of control over the gags, especially mechanical ones like the lift-and-ladder gag.

Classic Dialogue: Suggestively, Ollie says to Mae Busch: "I've never been in a position like that before..." "He who filters your good name steals trash," announces Stan.

Verdict: It would have been lovely to have seen Laurel and Hardy make more direct sequels to some of their films, although partial remakes and the fact that all the films take place in the same absurd world brought consistency. 3/5

The Fixer-Uppers

Director Charles Rogers. Two reels. Written & filmed January 1935. Released by MGM, February 1935. With Mae Busch, Charles Middleton, Arthur Housman, Noah Young

Story: Greeting-card salesmen Stan and Ollie encounter a woman upset by her husband's lack of affection. She engages Ollie to make a pass at her to spark her husband's jealousy. The plan works too well, and the husband challenges Ollie to a duel.

Production: A partial remake of *Slipping Wives* from 1927, *The Fixer-Uppers* appears to be set in Paris. A fire in the editing department at Hal Roach studios caused extensive damage and destroyed some footage from this film.

Classic Dialogue: Stan delivers one of his mangled tales: "When the husband found out the other fellow was jealous he took him in his arms, gave the wife a lot of money, then he kissed the other fella cause he made him jealous – and they all lived happily ever after!" Stan: "I'll have two beers, too." Stan: "If you had a face like mine, you'd punch me right on the nose."

L&H Moments: Stan pulls a great face as Mae Busch demonstrates how to kiss.

Verdict: It's another classic ("It sure is!") from a run of shorts when Laurel and Hardy were at the top of their form: just as the short film form itself was coming to an end. 3/5

Thicker Than Water

Director James Horne. Two reels. Written & filmed June-July 1935. Released by MGM, August 1935. With Daphne Pollard, James Finlayson, Charlie Hall, Bess Flowers

Working Title: Saturday Afternoon

Story: Stan is a boarder in the house of Mr and Mrs Hardy. After some bickering about rent payment, Stan talks Ollie into withdrawing the family savings in order to pay off their furniture. After withdrawing the money from the bank, Stan and Ollie happen by an auction house where they accidentally bid against each other on a grandfather clock and lose all the cash. The clock is destroyed by a passing truck. Mrs Hardy thumps Ollie with a frying pan. He is rushed to the hospital, in need of a transfusion. Stan donates his blood, and the boys end up sharing blood and exchanging personalities.

Production: Hal Roach was reluctant to abandon the production of short film comedies - they were easy and quick to make and brought great returns - but the film world had changed and feature films of one hour and over were now the norm. Stan Laurel may have hated the idea, but to continue working in pictures Laurel and Hardy had to adapt their style to features. Much of *Thicker Than Water* came from an abandoned feature-film script drafted by Stan Laurel, based on one of his own earlier comedy sketches. Never one to waste material, much of it was reused in *The Dancing Masters*.

Classic Dialogue: "Why, she talks to you like water off a duck's back," points out Stan, reasonably enough. Variation on a theme: "Well. Here's another nice kettle of fish you've pickled me in..."

L&H Moments: Dragging the screen wipes across the screen is a nice touch: it's neat that Laurel and Hardy acknowledge that they are in a film in their final short.

Verdict: At last, the boys get to play each other, the final culmination of playing each other's wives or children or their own twins. A fitting end to the short films – and the great James Finlayson's in it too. 3/5

10. The Classic Features, 1931-40

Pardon Us

Director James Parrott. 56 or 65 minutes. Written May-June 1930. Filmed June-July 1930, with retakes & new scenes filmed September-December. Released August 1931. With Walter Long, Wilfred Lucas, James Finlayson, Charlie Hall, Tiny Sandford

Working Title: The Rap (1930 preview prints), *Their First Mistake* (Jan 1931), *Jailbirds* (UK title)

Story: During prohibition, 'beer barons' Stan and Ollie are sent to prison for attempting to sell their own home brew to a policeman. They are put in a cell with 'Tiger' Long, the jail's meanest inmate. After a prison break, The boys escape to a cotton plantation, where they hide out. Discovered when they attempt to repair the warden's car, they are sent back to prison. Inadvertently Stan and Ollie break up a prison riot and the grateful warden issues a pardon.

Production: Although Laurel and Hardy were by far Roach's most popular performers and although the studio would make more money by putting them in features than by producing shorts, Roach was reluctant. He felt it was harder to sustain original comedy over 60 minutes and that a 20-minute two-reeler was the ideal length. Stan Laurel agreed, and he resisted attempts to move production over to seven-reel features.

Hal Roach obtained the use of the gigantic prison sets MGM had used for *The Big House*. However, the cost of rental ensured that the film, which was planned as a short, would not make a profit unless it was expanded to feature length. New sequences were constructed during production, and many added after the film had been previewed in 1930 under the title *The Rap*.

Laurel dipped into his back catalogue, raiding *Leave 'Em Laughing* (the dentist scenes) and *The Hoose-Gow* (fixing the Governor's car). Even then, Laurel wasn't happy with the 70-minute version of *The Rap*, cutting a further 14 minutes and developing the cotton-picking sequences. One sequence he cut (since restored) saw Stan and Ollie rescue the Warden's daughter from a fire.

After completing the revised film, Laurel and Hardy had to shoot it four more times for foreign language release, with *Pardon Us* becoming *Sous Les Verrous* in French (featuring Boris Karloff in the Walter Long role), *Hinter Schloss Unr Riegel* in German, *Muraglie* in Italian and *De Bote en Bote* in Spanish. Retained in the foreign remakes was a scene cut from the American release of Stan and Ollie as old men telling the story of their jailbreak to children. Prohibition didn't exist in Europe so the boys' crime was changed to investing stolen money.

Pardon Us took six months to make, on and off, and despite the reluctance of Laurel, Hardy and Roach, the film made so much money at the box office it was clear that they would be making more feature films.

Classic Dialogue: After having his prison mug shot taken, Stan asks: "If they turn out good, can I have one?" During James Finlayson's class Stan claims that a blizzard is "the inside of a buzzard."

L&H Moments: Old favourite routines revived here include the dentist visit, the loose tops on the salt-and-pepper joke and the bunk-bed routine from *Berth Marks*.

Verdict: This spoof of Warner Brothers jail movies of the 1930s is spot on, even with the dubious blacking-up required for Stan and Ollie to hide out on the happiest plantation in America's South! The restored scenes make *Pardon Us* more of a true feature, wrapping up some key story elements, although they don't add much to the comedy. As an accidental feature film, this was a good feature debut for Laurel and Hardy. 4/5

Pack Up Your Troubles

Directors George Marshall & Raymond McCarey. 68 minutes. Written April, 1932. Filmed May-June 1932. Released September 1932. With Donald Dillaway, Jacquie Lyn, George Marshall, James Finlayson, Rychard Cramer, Charles Middleton, Tom Kennedy, Frank Brownlee, Billy Gilbert

Story: It is 1917, America has just entered World War I. Stan and Ollie are drafted and create havoc in training camp and on the front line. Their friend Eddie Smith is killed in action. Upon their discharge, Stan and Ollie search for Eddie's orphaned daughter's grandparents, with the family name of Smith as their only lead.

Production: Although credited to both George Marshall and Ray McCarey (Leo's brother), it appears only Marshall worked on this. Producer Hal Roach insisted on the inclusion of Jacquie Lyn, the three-year-old who played Eddie Smith's daughter, believing he could develop her as a child star. The script was expanded to give her more screen time. Laurel's daughter, Lois, was originally slated to play the part, but it was felt she looked too old by the time filming started.

The 160th Tank Corps of Salinas, California, provided the vintage World War I tank, while the extras for the scenes were real soldiers who'd seen action in the 1914-1918 war. When the actor didn't show up, director George Marshall ended up playing the part of the surly cook who tells Stan and Ollie to take the garbage to the General. This improvisation led Laurel to devise the jail scene with Marshall and to include his character at the climax.

In 1994 *Pack Up Your Troubles* was shown in its original uncut form for the first time since its release in 1932. Scenes with Rychard Cramer as a child-and-wife-beating foster father were deemed so unpleasant, they were edited from all re-release prints. The scenes show a harder, more heroic edge to Stan and Ollie.

Classic Dialogue: Stan, hearing someone is incapacitated, comments: "There's been a lot of it going around..." Stan: "It was so dark, I didn't think you'd hear me."

L&H Moments: The boys share a bed, even on the front line, and maintain their domestic routines. Stan combs his hair with a fork.

Verdict: Another over-the-top James Finlayson moustache! Rather episodic, but charming (the girl Stan and Ollie look after) and serious (the issues of domestic violence and race are raised), this could have been a template for a series of contemporary Laurel and Hardy films, if they hadn't been sidetracked into 'operettas.' 4/5

Fra Diavolo

Directors Hal Roach & Charles Rogers. Script completed January 1933. Filmed February-March 1933. Released May 1933. With Dennis King, Thelma Todd, James Finlayson, Henry Armetta, Arthur Pierson, Lucille Brown, James C Morton

Alternative Title: The Devil's Brother

Story: In the early 18th century, northern Italy is terrorised by a notorious gang of thieves led by Fra Diavolo, 'The Devil's Brother.' Wanderers Stanlio and Ollio are held up by a band of Diavolo's men, and lose their life savings. They begin a life of crime, and bungle a series of robbery attempts with Ollio posing as the dreaded Diavolo. When they make the mistake of holding up the real Diavolo, he makes them his personal servants. Diavolo is enamoured with the charms of the lovely Lady Rocberg and the 500,000 francs she has hidden in her petticoat. Stan and Ollie help to expose Diavolo.

Production: Laurel and Hardy's first period operetta. When Hal Roach saw how well Laurel and Hardy had supported opera star Lawrence Tibbett in *The Rogue Song*, he wanted his top comics in their own operetta. Though Laurel and Hardy were initially sceptical about the project, this eventually became one of their favourite films.

Fra Diavolo provided a template for Laurel and Hardy feature films. Each of their scenes was designed as a self-contained comic sequence, structuring the film as a series of shorts tied together by the overall plot carried by the 'straight' actors. After previews, 27 minutes of Roach-directed plot was cut, emphasising the remaining comedy material directed by Charles Rogers.

All American prints carry the title *The Devil's Brother*, while European audiences, more familiar with the 1812 Auber source operetta, saw it under its original title of *Fra Diavolo*.

Classic Dialogue: Stan has to repeat his plan, and gets it hilariously wrong: "If we became rich, we could rob the poor and give it to the bandits. We could start at the top and get to the bottom without having to work hard anymore. It's the law of conversation!" Stan: "I don't want to walk around with my throat cut."

L&H Moments: Stan is credited as 'X' on the titles, recalling all those hotel guest books. Stan and Ollie end up crying when attempting a robbery and finally hand over their own money. Stan's finger wiggle and 'kneesy-earsy-nosey' game still fascinate child and adult audiences today.

Verdict: Best of the silly musical films, as the characters of Stan and Ollie fit the scenario better and it's also easier to ignore the tedious and dated songs. 3/5

Sons Of The Desert

Director William A Seiter. 68 minutes. Written July-September 1933. Filmed October 1933. Released December 1933. With Mae Busch, Dorothy Christie, Charlie Chase, Lucien Littlefield

Story: Stan and Ollie have taken a vow to attend the international convention of the Sons Of The Desert in Chicago. Their wives demand the boys take them on vacation to the mountains. Ollie fakes an illness for which the only cure is an ocean voyage. He and Stan announce they are setting sail for Hawaii, but sneak off to the convention. The wives are distraught when they receive word that the liner has sunk. Stan and Ollie are exposed when the wives see newsreel footage of the Sons Of The Desert convention, featuring their husbands playing to the cameras. After hiding out in the attic and on the roof, Stan and Ollie confront their wives. Ollie attempts to maintain the ruse, but Stan tells the truth. Stan's reward for his honesty is an evening of romantic bliss with his wife; Ollie, on the other hand, is the recipient of various flying projectiles aimed at his head.

Production: With two months to prepare *Sons Of The Desert*, Stan Laurel was determined that the new story would avoid some of the episodic elements of *Pardon Us* and *Pack Up Your Troubles*. Working closely with RKO director William A Seiter, Laurel ensured that the gags and plot were seamlessly integrated. It was through Seiter that Laurel would meet his second wife, Virginia Ruth Rogers.

Like the shorts, the film was shot almost in sequence, beginning with the scenes in the Hardy home in October 1933. The newsreel sequence was the last shot, with 500 extras employed to march along the updated Roach Studios New York street backlot.

Classic Dialogue: "That's the third apple missing this week," says Mrs Hardy of Stan's wax fruit eating. Stan: "Life isn't short enough." Ollie: "Well, if I have to go to Honolulu alone, he's coming with me!" Ollie: "I know she went out, but I'd like to know where did she went!" Stan: "We floundered in a typhoid."

Verdict: If the vet at the beginning had been James Finlayson, this film would have been perfect. Nonetheless, it's a classic Laurel and Hardy feature which bears repeated viewing thanks to the magic of the central performances and the natural fit of the situation to the boy's style of comedy. 5/5

Babes In Toyland

Directors Charles Rogers & Gus Meins. 79 minutes. Original script by Hal Roach, December 1933. Final script completed July 1934. Filmed February, August-October 1934. Released November 1934. With Charlotte Henry, Felix Knight, Henry Brandon, Florence Roberts, William Burress, Kewpie Morgan

Alternative Title: March Of The Wooden Soldiers

Story: Evil Silas Barnaby wants to evict Widow Peep from her giant shoe and marry her innocent daughter Bo Peep. He is thwarted at every turn by the efforts of toy-factory employees Stannie Dee and Ollie Dum, leading to a battle between Barnaby's Bogeymen and an army of six-foot-tall wooden soldiers.

Production: Babes In Toyland almost didn't get made. Hal Roach bought the rights to Victor Herbert's plotless operetta in late 1933, and drafted his own screenplay with the intention of turning it into a big-budget, all-star production. Stan Laurel rejected Roach's script, so the project was shelved for months.

Laurel's troubled private life may have affected his reluctance to commit to the film: he'd been divorced from Lois and was trying to avoid alimony. In fact, he'd considered leaving the US and breaking up the Laurel and Hardy partnership. Thankfully, that didn't happen, although there were no Laurel and Hardy film productions from February to May 1934 while Laurel solved his problems. He also got remarried, to Virginia Ruth Rogers in Mexico in April. His marriage was not recognised as legal in California as his divorce from Lois would not be final until October 1934. Hal Roach was far from happy with this state of affairs.

Similarly, Oliver Hardy was having a tough time. His wife Myrtle had been committed to an alcoholic's sanatorium in early 1934 because her drinking had increased. While spending more time with his close friend Viola Morse, Hardy didn't feel he could divorce Myrtle. During the hiatus in making the Laurel and Hardy films, Hardy was often to be found at the racetrack or playing golf.

All of this meant that *Going Bye-Bye* and *Them Thar Hills* saw production before the team returned to the idea of making *Babes In Toyland* as a feature film. June 1934 saw a new script in place and the Roach all-star approach dropped. Boasting some of the more extensive and imaginative sets seen in a Laurel and Hardy production, Laurel lamented that the film wasn't made in colour. Arguments over the script continued as the film entered production, but they proved academic as Laurel quickly reverted to his usual habit of developing funny business once on the soundstage. One week into shooting, Laurel suffered a fall and ended up with his leg in plaster. The film ground to a halt until he recovered.

Back in production in September 1934, the fights between Laurel and Roach over the comedy content continued, with Laurel winning most of the arguments. The released film won rave reviews, though. *Variety* called *Babes In Toyland* a "film of excellence for children." Despite that, the production of the film caused a rift in the Laurel-Roach relationship.

All current prints of the film carry its re-release title *March Of The Wooden Soldiers*, and runs nine minutes shorter than the original 1934 release.

Classic Dialogue: Stan: "You can't turn blood into a stone." Stan, again: "Her talking to Barnaby is just a matter of pouring one ear into another and coming out the other side. It just can't be done." Stan: "Upset? I'm housebroken!"

Verdict: Twee in many places, this is a Laurel and Hardy film aimed squarely at children, unlike most of the rest of their output. The Stan and Ollie characters are buried in the fairy-tale schmaltz and the incredibly hackneyed melodrama at the film's centre was old-fashioned even in 1934. Perhaps Hal Roach was right in this case... 2/5

Bonnie Scotland

Director James Horne. 80 minutes. Written January, April-May 1935. Filmed May-July 1935. Released August 1935. With June Lang, William Janney, Anne Grey, James Finlayson, David Torrence, Daphne Pollard

Working Titles: Kilts, Laurel And Hardy In India, McLaurel And McHardy

Story: Escaped convicts McLaurel and Hardy stow away to Scotland aboard a cattle boat in order to collect an inheritance from Stan's grandfather, the late Angus McLaurel. They get a snuffbox and a set of bagpipes. Penniless, they are reduced to cooking a fish over the bedsprings in their room at an inn. Evicted for destroying the room and failure to pay rent, they wander into an army recruiting line and wind up with a regiment in India. They encounter the evil Khan Mir Jutra, who plans to conquer the Scottish fort. He is thwarted when Stan and Ollie upset a number of beehives during the attack.

Production: The split between Laurel and Roach intensified. Trouble over story led to Laurel being fired according to a *Variety* report from 16 March 1935. Laurel's contract was due to expire in May, but Roach terminated it in March, vowing to replace the Laurel and Hardy shorts with a new series called *The Hardy Family*, featuring Hardy, Patsy Kelly and child star Spanky McFarland. Hardy's contract was up in November 1935. Neither Laurel nor Hardy wanted to break up their partnership. It was 8 April before a settlement was agreed, bringing Laurel back to the studio for one short and one feature, then six four-reel films over the next year. The new contract formalised the Laurel-Roach relationship as a business one rather than a personal one.

Production began on *Bonnie Scotland*, with James Finlayson returning to Laurel and Hardy after spending two years working in films and on stage in Britain. Filming was wrapped in six weeks, but previews revealed there was too much plot and not enough comedy. The film was recut and an extra 10 minutes of Stan and Ollie gag scenes were added, with the result that the plot makes little sense and the romantic sub-plot is left entirely unresolved.

Classic Dialogue: "I'll give you the room, but you'll have to take the bath yourself," replies landlady Mary Gordon when the boys ask for a room and a bath. Ollie: "Once again, I have to come to your rescue and be the mother of invention." Stan: "I've got an idea better than your mother's invention."

L&H Moments: Presenting their police prints and mug shots as proof of identity. Accidentally joining the army while in pursuit of a free suit.

Verdict: Plot-wise it may be a mess, but *Bonnie Scotland* delivers the laughs and contains the single best Laurel and Hardy sequence: the dance they break into while collecting litter which ends with them marching straight into a jail cell. 3/5

The Bohemian Girl

Directors James Horne & Charles Rogers. 70 minutes. Written July 1934, August-September 1935. Filmed October 1935-January 1936. Released February 1936. With Mae Busch, Antonio Moreno, Jacqueline Wells, Darla Hood, James Finlayson, Thelma Todd

Story: Stan and Ollie are part of a gypsy camp near the estate of Count Arnheim. Mrs Hardy makes no secret of her affair with the handsome Devilshoof. When Count Arnheim has Devilshoof flogged for trespassing, Mrs Hardy kidnaps the Count's daughter in revenge. She runs off with Devilshoof, leaving Ollie believing he is the girl's father. She is raised by Stan and Ollie. Years later, the gypsy band is again camped outside the Arnheim estate. The Count recognises his daughter, but not in time to save her kindly guardians from being squashed and stretched.

Production: Although planning a four-reel comedy entitled *The Honesty Racket* about FBI agents, Stan Laurel found himself working on another operetta after the commercial success of *Babes In Toyland*, even though he was reluctant to make something similar.

Hal Roach seemed more interested in the drama and music sequences of the Laurel and Hardy films, forgetting that they were meant to be comedies. He was scheduled to direct the 'straight' material, with James Horne handling the comedy. The fact that it was standard practice in these films for one director to do the operetta and another to do the comedy points up just why the finished films can seem so disjointed. Thankfully, Roach stayed away from the camera and Horne shared the direction with Charles Rogers.

On 16 December 1935, just five days after this film was previewed, Thelma Todd was found dead in her car in the garage, an apparent suicide. She was only 30 years old. Although her name remains in the credits, her role as the gypsy queen was cut from the film when Roach and Laurel agreed they didn't want her death connected with the movie. Due to its gypsy content, *The Bohemian Girl* was banned by the Nazis in Germany.

Upset by the preference of Hal Roach for operetta material which did not suit Laurel and Hardy, and with his previous threats to break up the partnership, Laurel decided he needed more control over the next film and so established Stan Laurel Productions.

Classic Dialogue: Stan tries fortune-telling: "I see a long woman and a dark journey." Stan exclaims amazement with: "Blow me down with an anchovy." Stan calculates the time to make a malted milk: "About 15 minutes to a quarter of an hour."

L&H Moments: During Stan's wine bottling, he drinks as much as he bottles and ends up blotto.

Verdict: Too much music and singing - with three musical numbers in the first 15 minutes. The Laurel and Hardy material is great, but it is swamped with all the gypsy song-and-dance nonsense... a sign of worse things to come. 3/5

Our Relations

A Stan Laurel Production for Hal Roach Studios. Director Harry Lachman. 74 minutes. Written February-March 1936. Filmed March-May 1936. Released October 1936. With James Finlayson, Daphne Pollard, Betty Healy, Alan Hale, Sidney Toler, Iris Adrian, Lona Andre

Story: Stan and Ollie each have an identical twin brother, a fact they keep secret from their wives out of fear that they'd be divorced. The twins, Alf and Bert, are sailors who arrive in town on leave. Confusion reigns as each set of twins is mistaken for the other. The truth is eventually discovered, and the twins enjoy a happy, if rather wet, reunion.

Production: By 1936, with the shorts a distant memory and the dominance of feature-film production certain, Stan Laurel felt he was better qualified than producer Hal Roach to decide what constituted a Laurel and Hardy film. To that end, both *Our Relations* and *Way Out West* became 'Stan Laurel Productions,' even though Laurel was still under personal contract to Roach, a contract which had been extended for another year. It seems that Roach saw the sense in giving Laurel the kind of creative control he'd had on the shorts (Laurel was now an actor and writer with story and director approval) and the result was two of the best Laurel and Hardy feature films.

Laurel turned to the short story *The Money Box* by William Wymark Jacobs as source material and hired a new director and director of photography, Harry Lachman and Rudolph Maté (who'd collaborated on the 1935 Spencer Tracy film *Dante's Inferno*). Despite hiring talented people, Laurel was still directing and creating the film by default, a fact which caused friction between him, Lachman and Maté.

It seems Laurel and Hardy had some powerful fans. *Our Relations* was screened before release at Balmoral Castle in Scotland as a Royal Command Performance for King Edward VIII. US President Roosevelt also requested a private screening of the film.

Classic Dialogue: "Captain, you can trust us insipidly," insists Ollie. Stan, about their wives: "We'll give them enough rope so we can hang ourselves." Mrs Hardy instructs Mrs Laurel on answering the phone: "If that's them, tell them we're not home." Ollie explains his and Stan's ridiculous get-up: "We're a couple of Singapore Eskimos." Stan to his twin Alf: "You've altered too, but you haven't changed a bit."

L&H Moments: Ollie sees perfectly well through glasses with no glass.

Verdict: Fantastic! This has the potential to be extremely confusing and indulgent, but it is well orchestrated so the audience knows exactly who is who at any given moment. The material plays to the characters strengths and nothing detracts from the Laurel and Hardy we expect to see – and no songs! 5/5

On The Wrong Trek

Directors Charles Parrott & Harold Law. Two reels. Written & filmed mid-late April 1936. Released mid-June 1936. With Charley Chase, Rosina Lawrence

Story: Charley Chase and family take a fraught car trip to California.

Production: This was Chase's penultimate film for Roach and came near the end of production of the two-reelers. Laurel and Hardy were invited to play a very brief cameo as one set of many hitch-hikers encountered by Chase on his cross-country drive.

L&H Moments: The boys are hitch-hiking in opposite directions (later reused in *A Haunting We Will Go*).

Verdict: Laurel and Hardy as a quick sight gag: blink and you'll miss 'em. 1/5

Way Out West

A Stan Laurel Production for Hal Roach Studios. Director James Horne. 65 minutes. Written May-August 1936. Filmed August-November 1936. Released by MGM, April 1937. With James Finlayson, Rosina Lawrence, Sharon Lynne, Stanley Fields, Vivien Oakland

Working Title: In The Money

Story: Stan and Ollie arrive in Brushwood Gulch to deliver a mine deed to Mary Roberts, bequeathed by her late father. Never having seen Mary Roberts, the boys are duped by Fin, a shifty saloon owner, into thinking his wife Lola is Mary. They turn over the deed to the crooks, but realise their mistake when they encounter the real Mary. Breaking into the saloon at night to recover the deed, they wreck the place, put their mule on the roof, hang Fin from a chandelier and succeed in their mission.

Production: Stan Laurel's wife, Ruth, suggested the idea of a comedy western for the next Laurel and Hardy feature film. Unlike the previous 'operetta' films, the music in *Way Out West* was firmly part of the film. The soft-shoe shuffle to the Avalon Boys rendition of the 1905 hit *At The Ball, That's All* was created during shooting, but serves the characters of Stan and Ollie far better than any opera nonsense. The famous version of *The Trail Of The Lonesome Pine* was another addition during shooting and proved to be one of the most widely appreciated of Laurel and Hardy's musical moments. The entire number was recorded live on set, except for the dubbing of Laurel's low and high voices (provided by Chill Wills and Rosina Lawrence respectively). In 1975 the track was released as a single in the UK, astonishingly reaching number 2 in the charts. Also invented on the set was Stan lighting his thumb as if it were a match, which also became one of Laurel and Hardy's most famous gags. The film was nominated for an Oscar for Marvin Hatley's music score, but didn't win.

During shooting, Laurel was embroiled in another contract dispute with Hal Roach. His deal was coming to an end - Roach had Laurel and Hardy on separate contracts which came up for renewal at different times, ensuring he always had one or the other of his top stars under contract. Laurel felt that Roach needed him more than he needed Roach so held out in the middle of making *Way Out West* for a better settlement. The result was a proposed, but never signed, agreement for a two-year, four-film contract.

Also at this time, Laurel separated from his wife Ruth while his ex-vaudeville partner and one-time common law wife Mae Laurel resurfaced claiming maintenance. Hardy's wife Myrtle sued for divorce, forcing him to testify about her drinking and visits to sanatoriums. Both Myrtle Hardy and Ruth Laurel were represented by the same lawyer, suggesting a degree of opportunism. During the same period, Hardy's first wife Madelyn reappeared, claiming to be destitute in New York and chasing him for maintenance for the past 15 years. Somehow, both comedians managed to keep smiling and all the cases were settled over the next year. Hal Roach, however, was none too pleased at the public reputation his star comedians were attracting.

Classic Dialogue: "A lot of weather we've been having lately," says Ollie making polite conversation on the coach. When asked what Mary Robert's father died of, Stan says: "I think he died of a Tuesday, or was it a Wednesday...?"

Verdict: Two in a row: this is Laurel and Hardy at their best. Even the songs are integrated to their characters and involve the boys instead of being a distraction from the comedy business at hand. If only there could have been more features with Laurel in charge like this one... 5/5

Pick A Star

Director Edward Sedgwick. 70 minutes. Written Summer 1936. Filmed November 1936 & January 1937. Released May 1937. With Patsy Kelly, Jack Haley, Rosina Lawrence, Lyda Roberti, Mischa Auer

Story: An aspiring singer comes to Hollywood to try her luck in the movies, with her wisecracking sister in tow.

Production: Laurel and Hardy took one day out, on 16 November 1936, from shooting *Way Out West* to film guest scenes for Hal Roach's forthcoming musical comedy *Pick A Star*. In the first of two scenes, they are shooting a western with Walter Long under the direction of James Finlayson. They explain the use of special movie prop bottles to Nellie (Patsy Kelly) who is visiting the studio with a graphic (and for Ollie, painful) demonstration. In the second scene, the boys are fooling around with some musical instruments, including a mouth organ and a toy horn.

L&H Moments: Stan discovers he can play *Pop Goes The Weasel* on Ollie's stomach after Ollie swallows a tiny mouth organ.

Verdict: It's nice to see the boys almost playing themselves in the studio scenes, while the musical scene is a bit of fun comedy not repeated elsewhere. A minor curiosity. 3/5

Swiss Miss

Director John G Blystone. 72 minutes. Written October-November 1937. Filmed December 1937-February 1938. Retakes & new scenes filmed April 1938. Released May 1938. With Walter Woolf King, Della Lind, Eric Blore, Charles Judels, Ludovico Tomarchio, Anita Garvin, Charles Gemora

Working Title: Swiss Cheese

Story: Mousetrap salesmen Stan and Ollie sell their wares in Switzerland (there's more cheese, you see) for phoney money. They celebrate with a lavish dinner at a fancy hotel but, unable to pay the bill, they are forced to work in the hotel's kitchen. Ollie falls in love with the hotel's chambermaid, who is a famous opera singer hiding out from her husband. The husband, Victor, is attempting to write a grand opera. Monkey business ensues.

Production: A year elapsed between *Way Out West* and *Swiss Miss*, during which time Stan Laurel was briefly reconciled and then separated again from wife Ruth while he negotiated contracts with Hal Roach. Laurel's contract had expired, but Hardy was still tied to Roach for another two years. Roach again threatened to put Hardy into other films alone. Laurel wanted to win back creative control of the Laurel and Hardy pictures, either by negotiating a better contract from Roach or working solo until Hardy was free, whereupon they could make Laurel and Hardy films under their own control. Laurel's company also served as a shelter for Laurel's earnings, protecting them from the attention of various ex-wives...

Finally, on 6 October 1937, Stan Laurel Productions (but not Laurel personally) signed a deal with Roach Studios for four films, allowing Laurel to produce other non-Roach films (a series of westerns). Laurel was employed as 'actor-performer-writer-director' at $2,500 per week and $25,000 per film for the next two years.

Roach concentrated on the drama and the music of *Swiss Miss*, believing the stars of the film to be Walter Woolf King and Della Lind, while Laurel felt he was making a comedy starring him and Hardy. The result is a disjointed film with too much music and too little comedy.

As shooting began Laurel married again, to Russian singer Vera Illiana Shuvalova, immediately after his divorce from Ruth was finalised (although Ruth publicly disputed this, calling Laurel a bigamist). Laurel had apparently 'screen-tested' Shuvalova for the part of Anna five weeks previously, but decided she was more suited to the role of Mrs Laurel. The headlines didn't help Laurel in his quest to win more creative control over his films.

Early scenes of *Swiss Miss* were shot in colour, before Roach decided it was too expensive and reverted to black and white midway through the first week. No colour footage of the movie has ever surfaced. Laurel did manage to assert control over one sequence in the film – and it turned out to be the most memorable. The whole 'Stan and Ollie haul a piano across a rope bridge' sequence was Laurel's creation.

Classic Dialogue: "We should get some fire and put the water out," advises Stan. "I'll try some of that demitasse and bring me a cup of coffee, too," says Stan, ever the sophisticate. "You're in love: L-U-G-H. Love!" says Stan of Ollie, before telling him the story of the "gay caviars." "The brother you haven't got wouldn't even know you," says Ollie of Stan's disguise: a fake moustache which would shame James Finlayson. "We're not us, we're two other fellows," insists Stan, as the chef sees through his disguise.

L&H Moments: Stan develops a deep voice once again and the boys get to do a dish-washing dance. The sequence where they rub out the days due to be worked on the blackboard is magic.

Verdict: Instead of a dull operetta with Laurel and Hardy shoe-horned in, we get a dull composer writing an operetta! Again, there are too many dire musical numbers and not enough Laurel and Hardy comedy, although the reprise of *The Music Box* and *The Chimp* is welcome. There is one classic scene, where Stan dupes a St Bernard dog so he can drink its emergency brandy. Regular supporting actors like James Finlayson and Charlie Hall are sorely missed. Additionally, Hardy looks bigger and Laurel older... the decline starts here. 3/5

Block-Heads

Director John G Blystone. 58 minutes. Written May-June 1938. Filmed June-July 1938. Released August 1938. With Minna Gombell, Billy Gilbert, Patricia Ellis, James Finlayson

Working Titles: Meet The Missus, Just A Jiffy

Story: Private Stan Laurel is discovered patrolling the trenches 20 years after the end of World War I. Old pal Oliver Hardy reads about Stan in the papers, and visits him at the Old Soldier's Home. Ollie invites Stan home for a steak dinner.

Mrs Hardy storms out, so Stan and Ollie attempt to cook their own meal. They blow up the kitchen, and a partial remake of *Unaccustomed As We Are* follows.

Production: For 11 years, Roach Studios had distributed their films through MGM. In 1938 Roach signed a new deal with United Artists, but still owed MGM one film under the old contract. A quick and cheap Laurel and Hardy feature was required. Hurried and chaotic, filming proceeded at a time when Laurel and Roach were not on the best of terms, and Laurel's personal problems with his third (official) wife Illiana distracted him. In addition, both Laurel and Hardy were nearing the end of their respective Roach contracts, and there were strong rumours that this would be their last film. Despite the problems, *Block-Heads* emerged as one of their better features, even if it is a combination of bits from *Pack Up Your Troubles*, a remake of *Unaccustomed As We Are* and a scene lifted from *We Faw Down*.

Harry Langdon, a one-time successful film comedian now struggling at Roach Studios, was hired by Laurel as a gag man and he worked with Laurel for the next two years, from *Block-Heads* to *Saps At Sea*. Shooting on *Block-Heads* took a month, with Laurel absent much of the time and (according to Roach) often drunk or drinking on set. Laurel's marriage to Illiana was proving as stormy as his previous liaisons, resulting in newspaper reports of domestic disturbances. Just four days after completion of the final cut, the film's 45-year-old director (and director of *Swiss Miss*) John G Blystone died on 6 August of a heart attack. On 12 August, the same night of the press preview of *Block-Heads*, Roach Studios terminated Laurel's contract. Roach told the press that Harry Langdon would be replacing Laurel in partnership with Oliver Hardy for the two remaining films on Laurel's contract. Composer Marvin Hatley was nominated for an Oscar for *Block-Heads* for Best Original Score of 1938, but didn't win.

Classic Dialogue: "If I hadn't seen you, I wouldn't have known you," says Stan of Ollie. "A knick-knack is a thing that sits on top of a what-not," explains the ever-helpful Ollie.

L&H Moments: Ollie thinks Stan has lost a leg (he's sitting in a wheelchair with one leg tucked under him) and then carries him to the car. Stan's hand doubles as a pipe and he has a self-igniting match.

Verdict: A troubled production, but a fine – if overly familiar – film. Billy Gilbert and James Finlayson make welcome appearances and the whole thing appears very modern. There are nice details, like the hole where Stan has been turning in the trench and the pile of discarded cans, but *Block-Heads* is no classic. 3/5

A Chump At Oxford

Director Alfred Goulding. 42 minutes/63 minutes. Written April-May 1939. Filmed June 1939 (42-minute version). New scenes written & filmed September 1939 (63-minute version). Released by United Artists, February 1940. With Forrester Harvey, Wilfred Lucas, Forbes Murray, Eddie Borden, James Finlayson, Anita Garvin, Peter Cushing, Charlie Hall

Story: After their jobs as butler and maid at a lavish dinner party proves a disaster, Stan and Ollie end up sweeping the streets. They foil a bank robbery and are offered an education at Oxford University as a reward. At Oxford, they are the victims of a series of practical jokes by other students. When Stan bumps his head, he changes personalities to become Lord Paddington, the great scholar and athlete. He makes Ollie his manservant. Another bump on the head causes Stan to recover.

Production: In September 1938 it was announced by film producer Mack Sennett (an old rival to Hal Roach) that he'd signed Stan Laurel to star in his film *Problem Child*, the tale of the normal-sized son of midget parents. The film was never made, and may have never been intended to be made: Sennett had been retired for five years and Laurel was using the proposed film as a bargaining chip with Roach. It might have worked if Laurel hadn't spent a night in jail after a further domestic disturbance and a drink-and-driving charge. Meanwhile, Oliver Hardy was busy making *Zenobia* with Harry Langdon and an elephant.

By the middle of 1939, Illiana was an ex-Mrs Laurel. Embroiled in legal conflicts with the Roach Studios, it was only the failure of Hardy's *Zenobia* at the box office that brought Laurel back to the team. A one-year contract was signed between Laurel and Roach in April 1939 - Hardy also signed to a simultaneous one-year contract. Although the boys were not under a joint contract, their commitments to Roach now ran in parallel, something Laurel had wanted for some time. At the same time, Roach agreed to loan Laurel and Hardy out to independent producer Boris Morros to star in his proposed film *The Flying Deuces*, to start shooting in July.

The new film for Roach was to be a streamlined 42-minute, four-reel format. It was hoped that removing the padding that had afflicted some of the team's features, they'd return to their former comedic heights. The director was Alf Goulding, an ex-vaudeville colleague of Laurel's who'd originally introduced him to Hal Roach in 1918. Among the students playing pranks on the boys were familiar faces Charlie Hall and a very young Peter Cushing, over a decade before he found fame in Hammer's horror movies.

Filming completed, Laurel and Hardy went off to film *The Flying Deuces*. Roach, however, decided he wanted a longer version of *A Chump At Oxford* for European release, so in September 1939, Laurel and Hardy shot their first two-reeler on the Roach lot since 1935's *Thicker Than Water*. This remake of *From*

Soup To Nuts was added to the front of the film, bringing the running time up to 63 minutes.

Classic Dialogue: "We're not illiterate enough," says Stan, lamenting his and Ollie's lack of education. "He's got bees in his cockpit," says Stan of someone who's crazy. Ollie gets a fantastic aside to himself: "If it wasn't for that bump on the head, he wouldn't know Einstein from a beer stein!"

L&H Moments: Stan manages to finger wiggle with three hands.

Verdict: Another poor remake leads into the tiresome maze and 'ghost' scenes. The fact that all Stan and Ollie's problems are due to student pranks seems to detract from their usual comic struggle with life. It all seems a bit malicious. 2/5

The Flying Deuces

Producer Boris Morros. Director Edward Sutherland. 69 minutes. Written April-May 1939. Filmed July-August 1939. Released by RKO-Radio Pictures, October 1939. With Jean Parker, Charles Middleton, Reginald Gardiner, James Finlayson

Story: Stan and Ollie are in Paris, where Ollie falls in love with the innkeeper's daughter. He discovers she is already married and decides to jump in the river, with Stan in tow. A French Foreign Legion officer talks Stan and Ollie out of suicide and into joining the Legion. They enlist, wreak havoc in the training camp, and are arrested for desertion. They escape by stealing an airplane, which crash-lands. Ollie is reincarnated as a horse.

Production: The only film from Laurel and Hardy's vintage days to have been produced by someone other than Hal Roach. After throwing out a first script by Alfred Schiller (based on a French film *Les Aviateurs*), Laurel reunited the writers of *Block-Heads* and *A Chump At Oxford* – Langdon, Charles Rogers and himself – to script *The Flying Deuces*. In Laurel's hands, the film became a remake of *Beau Hunks* and used the proposed suicide material drafted for *The Live Ghost*. Ironically, away from the Roach Studios, Laurel found the control over material he had been looking for. However, he found working with director Edward Sutherland to be difficult. Sutherland was also on a loan-out from Roach Studios and wasn't keen on handling a Laurel and Hardy film, so there was friction during the production. Laurel provided copious notes about the editing after seeing a first rough cut, only to have them ignored by the editors. Laurel and Hardy would only make one more film with Hal Roach.

Classic Dialogue: "Don't talk to me like that after all the hospital I've given you!" complains Dr Stan. "I'd rather come back as myself. I always got on swell with me," says Stan while discussing reincarnation. "I wouldn't bother leaving him a note. Just leave him a PS – that's good enough for him," says Stan of Camp Commandant Charles Middleton. Stan hates flying, preferring to be on "good old terracotta."

Verdict: Two great musical numbers – Ollie singing *Harvest Moon* and Stan turning his bed springs into a harp – aren't enough to raise this *Beau Hunks* remake above average for most of the running time. There is one classic scene, and Laurel and Hardy ain't in it: it's when Fin watches the Legion march into a cell, vanish and then reappear drunk (including a briefly-glimpsed Arthur Housman). 3/5

Saps At Sea

Director Gordon Douglas. 57 minutes. Written September-October 1939. Filmed November-December 1939. Released by United Artists, May 1940. With Rychard Cramer, James Finlayson, Eddie Conrad, Robert McKenzie, Harry Bernard, Charlie Hall, Ben Turpin

Working Titles: Two's Company, Jitterbugs, Crackpots

Story: Stan and Ollie are employees at a horn factory, where the constant honking drives Ollie to a nervous breakdown. An ocean voyage is the prescription for Ollie's condition, but he's afraid of the sea. They rent a boat and keep it tied to the dock. Escaped convict Nick Grainger sneaks aboard the boat, while the boys' pet goat eats through the mooring ropes, setting them adrift. In the morning, Grainger forces Stan and Ollie to prepare a meal. Having no food, they concoct a synthetic meal (string for spaghetti, sponges for meatballs, lamp wicks for bacon). When Grainger threatens their lives, Stan starts blowing his trombone which causes Ollie to go berserk and he overcomes Grainger.

Production: For the final Hal Roach Laurel and Hardy film, Laurel again formed the core of the scripting team, with Harry Langdon and Charles Rogers. The film appears to be two shorts lumped together, with the opening half-hour in an apartment and the final half-hour on the boat. The director was 30-year-old Gordon Douglas, who'd helmed *Zenobia*. Laurel also brought across the script girl from *The Flying Deuces*, Lucille Jones, who worked on the reshoots for *A Chump At Oxford* and on all of *Saps At Sea*, turning Langdon, Rogers and Laurel's jokes into a cohesive scenario. Her confirmation as a key player in Laurel and Hardy's final films came when she married Oliver Hardy in May 1940.

After *Saps At Sea* wrapped, the one-year contracts between Laurel, Hardy and Roach expired. Instead of delivering four four-reel comedies, the team had supplied two feature-length films. Laurel and Hardy were now free from Hal Roach and able to develop their own projects as an independent team. The first thing they did was a 12-city stage tour of the US, starting in September 1940, performing *The Laurel And Hardy Revue*. The packed houses and press reaction proved to the boys that their public appeal had not dimmed since their tour of the UK in 1932.

Classic Dialogue: "We must've been dis-unconnected," explains Stan of his phone troubles. "Do ghosts have milk?" asks Stan. "I don't give a continental!" is the entirely mysterious parting shot from James Finlayson in his final Laurel and Hardy appearance. "Take a hot bath and relapse," is Stan's wise medical advice. Stan questions nursery rhymes: "How can a dead dog smoke...?" Stan refuses to accept the boat is adrift: "Somebody moved the dock!"

Verdict: Last of the classics, and the last Laurel and Hardy to feature familiar faces like James Finlayson, Charlie Hall and Mary Gordon. The house appliances being all wrong comes straight from *Call Of The Cuckoo*, while the rest is equally unoriginal. The end of an era... 3/5

11. The Late Films, 1941-1954

Great Guns

Producer 20th Century-Fox, Sol M Wurtzel. Screenplay Lou Breslow. Director Montague 'Monty' Banks. 74 minutes. Written May-June 1941. Filmed July-August 1941. Released October 1941. With Dick Nelson, Sheila Ryan, Edmund MacDonald

Working Title: Marching Forward

Story: Stan and Ollie enlist to keep an eye on their sickly employer, Dan. Once in the Army, they manage to wreak havoc.

Production: As the 1940s dawned, both Laurel and Hardy were caught up in tax problems, with each owing the Government back taxes. Laurel's private life was no calmer as he remarried his ex-wife Ruth in January 1941 – a reunion which only lasted five months. Laurel and Hardy formed their own corporation, Laurel and Hardy Feature Productions, to make movies. They were approached by 20th Century-Fox and signed to make a one-off army comedy, with an option to make nine further films in a non-exclusive deal over five years at a fee of $50,000 per film. Laurel was happy to be working with a major studio, little realising that the sheer size of Fox meant that he'd have even less control over the Laurel and Hardy productions than he'd enjoyed at Roach.

The new studio set about reinventing Laurel and Hardy. Laurel was no longer allowed to use the white face paint which gave him his characteristic 'empty-faced' look. Instead, he'd be made up in the Fox style, a change which made Laurel suddenly look older. Similarly, Fox did away with the distinctive Laurel and Hardy look, deciding instead it would be funnier if Laurel's clothes were too big for him while Hardy's were too small.

That wasn't all: Laurel could not contribute to the storyline or script of the new film and had no influence on the director. He and Hardy were simply being hired as on-screen comics, not as the creative forces behind the film. Laurel began to realise that the Fox deal may have been a mistake. One example: on the Roach lot much of the comedy material was developed on the set, a working method only possible as shooting took place in sequence. At Fox, in common with standard feature-film production, scenes were shot out of order, making full use of specific sets. This production method inhibited Laurel's attempts to inject some of his comic talent into scenes and make the most of on-the-set inspiration. Laurel and Hardy lost their spontaneity – and much else besides.

Classic Dialogue: An exchange between Stan and another soldier: "Those are our eggs!" complains Stan. "Did you lay them?" asks the soldier. "Yes. I laid them on the tray just a minute ago!"

Verdict: First of the 1940s movies, where Laurel and Hardy were not the leads nor the protagonists in their own films, despite top billing. There's a lot of badly reused dialogue and material, including Stan at both ends of the plank from *The Finishing Touch* and the "we haven't eaten for three days" line from

One Good Turn. The Laurel and Hardy in the army scenario had been done several times before, so much better. 1/5

A Haunting We Will Go

Producer 20th Century-Fox, Sol M Wurtzel. Screenplay Lou Breslow. Director Alfred L Werker. 67 minutes. Written January-March 1942. Filmed March-April 1942. Released August 1942. With Dante the Magician (Harry A Jansen), Elisha Cook Jr., Sheila Ryan, Don Costello

Working Title: Pitfalls Of A Big City

Story: Run out of town by the cops, Stan and Ollie get caught up in a gangster caper and team up with a touring magician.

Production: While Laurel and Hardy embarked on a tour to entertain the Allied troops and then a stage tour of the US, the script for *A Haunting We Will Go* was being written, with no input from Stan. After the one-film deal for *Great Guns*, Laurel reluctantly agreed to continue with Fox. "I kept thinking that sooner or later they would let us do the pictures our own way," Laurel admitted, "but it just got worse."

During shooting, under humourless director Alfred Werker, there was no improvisation or straying from the approved script, meaning that Laurel and Hardy were unable to rescue the film by injecting some routines developed on the spot. Instead, they simply had to go through the motions and deliver out-of-character performances and dialogue. Even when old material was reworked, as in the rebuilt statue gag from *Wrong Again*, it's shot so badly and directed so limply that the gag just falls flat.

As soon as filming was over, Laurel and Hardy returned to a performing venue they were finding more rewarding than film: the stage. They joined the Hollywood Victory Caravan, an entertain-the-troops tour which featured big show-business names. Hal Roach, meanwhile, had joined up, becoming a lieutenant colonel. He leased the Roach Studios facility to the US Army to produce propaganda and training films. There was now no way back to Roach Studios for Laurel and Hardy even if they had wanted to return.

Classic Dialogue: Ollie: "It's better to spend one night with a corpse than 60 days with the cops." Ollie justifies his plans for using the Inflato currency machine: "We'd only make enough for our bare necessities." Stan whispers to him: "And a swimming pool..."

Verdict: Featuring tiresome magic routines rather than tiresome musical numbers and a doubtful gangster plot, this is nothing more than a Fox 1940s B-movie about criminal capers, with Laurel and Hardy shoe-horned in with very little thought or awareness of their characters. They're taken advantage of at every turn and lack that down-at-heel dignity they usually possess. As for Dante getting co-top billing: it's a travesty. There isn't even any haunting... 1/5

Air Raid Wardens

Producer BF Zeidman for MGM. Director Edward Sedgwick. Screenplay Charles Rogers, Jack Jevene, Martin Rackin & Harry Crane. 67 Minutes. Written September 1942. Filmed December 1942-January 1943. Released April 1943. With Edgar Kennedy, Horace McNally

Story: Rejected by each of the armed forces, Stan and Ollie become civil-defence air-raid wardens. Though they prove to be a hindrance to the war effort, they do capture a bunch of Nazi spies.

Production: As the contract with Fox was non-exclusive, Laurel and Hardy were free to make films for others. Although MGM were notorious for not allowing comics like Buster Keaton and the Marx Brothers to make films in their own way, Stan Laurel believed that enlisting some old hands from the Roach Studios days would help. As a result, Charles Rogers and Jack Jevene contributed to the script and Edgar Kennedy found himself back in front of the camera. Director Edward Sedgwick had worked with the boys before on the all-star comedy, *Pick A Star*.

Despite all this, *Air Raid Wardens* fell as flat as the attempt to rework situations with Edgar Kennedy from *Bacon Grabbers*. The tit-for-tat sequence with Kennedy should have been a highlight, harking back to past glory. Instead, it's a series of poor gags which don't build and aren't underlined by close-up reaction shots.

Around this time some old Laurel and Hardy shorts were being reissued to cinemas by MGM. Also in 1943, Laurel and Hardy recorded a pilot (with Edgar Kennedy) for a proposed radio show. Adapting their comedy to the audio medium proved difficult and the show wasn't picked up. A similar fate befell another radio pilot recorded in 1944 and a planned mid-1950s BBC radio comedy called *Laurel & Hardy Go To The Moon*.

Classic Dialogue: Stan: "Ollie, burglars!" Ollie (despondent): "I don't want any."

Verdict: There are glimpses here of the classic Laurel and Hardy characters, but that only serves to remind us of how good the boys used to be, and how unsuited they were to all these Abbott and Costello-style caper movies. The forced wartime patriotism doesn't help either. 2/5

Jitterbugs

Producer 20th Century-Fox, Sol M Wurtzel. Screenplay W Scott Darling. Director Malcolm St Clair. 74 minutes. Written February 1943. Filmed February-March 1943. Released by 20th Century-Fox June 1943. With Vivian Blaine, Bob Bailey, Douglas Fowley

Story: Stan and Ollie team up with a conman to outswindle some swindlers. In the process, Ollie gets to portray a Southern Colonel and Stan does a turn in drag.

Production: Fox producer Sol M Wurtzel found it difficult to come up with new vehicles for Laurel and Hardy. Rather than turn to Laurel or the team's back-catalogue for inspiration, Wurtzel tried *Boston Blackie* series scripter Paul Yawitz. His rejected script, entitled *Me And My Shadow*, involved Nazi spies, missing microfilm and mobsters. Another late 1942 script saw Stan and Ollie running a sanatorium in the Alps which is packed with secret agents. Wurtzel finally turned to a screenwriter who'd written comedies in the 1920s and, more recently, mysteries and dramas, like *The Ghost Of Frankenstein*: W Scott Darling. He also hired an experienced comedy director, Malcolm St Clair, who'd worked with Mack Sennett and Buster Keaton.

The boys play swing musicians, complete with attendant slang. By this stage, even Oliver Hardy was beginning to feel like their characters were afterthoughts in the Fox films. In a 1951 interview with the *LA Times* he commented: "The writers they brought in only wanted to write highbrow stuff: they couldn't be bothered with us." Laurel agreed: "It breaks your heart when they send you a script on a Friday night and say you're to start shooting Monday morning. We're not used to that kind of treatment."

Classic Dialogue: Stan: "I was just thinking..." Ollie: "What about?" Stan: "Nothing. I was just thinking."

Verdict: The opening of the film certainly has our boys in character, but it's downhill all the way from there. *Jitterbugs* sees the return of the dreaded musical numbers, but at least they are contemporary. Another in a series of bad films. 2/5

Tree In A Test Tube

Producer US Dept. of Agriculture, Forest Service. Director Charles McDonald. One reel. Colour. Filmed circa February-March 1943. Released Spring 1943. Narration by Peter Smith, Lee Vickers

Production: Laurel and Hardy's only surviving colour footage sees them empty a suitcase of ordinary items, while Pete Smith's jokey narration points out the wood content of each item and the role wood is playing in the war effort.

Verdict: A curiosity: the boys don't do much, but it's good to see them in colour for five minutes. 2/5

The Dancing Masters

Producer Lee Marcus. Screenplay W Scott Darling. Director Malcolm St Clair. 63 minutes. Written May 1943. Filmed June 1943. Released by 20th Century-Fox, November 1943. With Trudy Marshall, Bob Bailey, Margaret Dumont, Robert Mitchum

Story: Dancing teachers Stan and Ollie team up with a young woman and a young inventor to help raise funds for his new weapon: an invisible ray.

Production: Fox finally realised that the films were missing recognisable Laurel and Hardy routines. To rectify this, W Scott Darling took a draft script by

George Bricker called *A Matter Of Money* and shoe-horned in a dancing school, a pointless extortion racket and material from old Laurel and Hardy films: *Battle Of The Century*, *Thicker Than Water*, *Dirty Work*, *County Hospital* and *Block-Heads*. None of the gags or sequences were properly developed, properly paid off or made much sense in the context of the story, but at least they were recognisable as Laurel and Hardy routines.

Classic Dialogue: Stan: "We've all got to live and learn." Ollie: "You just live!" Stan: "The harder they fall, the bigger I am." Stan: "You can't keep an egg in two baskets, unless you scramble them..."

Verdict: A curiosity, as much for the scene the boys share with Robert Mitchum and the appearance of the Marx Brothers' foil Margaret Dumont rather than any Laurel and Hardy comedy business. 3/5 (but only for the original source material)

The Big Noise

Producer Sol M Wurtzel. Screenplay W Scott Darling. Director Malcolm St Clair. 74 minutes. Written December 1943. Filmed March-April 1944. Released by 20th Century-Fox, October 1944. With Arthur Space, Robert 'Bobby' Blake

Working Title: Good Neighbours

Story: Janitors Stan and Ollie pass themselves off as detectives to be hired by an eccentric inventor, who wants them to protect his new explosive (dubbed 'the big noise') powerful enough to blow up a city. After several complications (and remakes of earlier shorts), the boys drop the bomb on a Japanese submarine.

Production: Once again, writer W Scott Darling took a standard 1940s propaganda film about crooks, Nazis and patriotic inventors and added gags from a seemingly random selection of old Laurel and Hardy shorts (*Habeas Corpus*, *Wrong Again*, *Oliver The Eighth*). Stan Laurel wanted the old material to be updated to reflect the 1940s rather than the 1920s or 1930s. For example, he wanted to rework the train sequence from *Berth Marks* on an aeroplane. Fox said no, wanting to recreate the gags as quickly and cheaply as possible. Oliver Hardy reintroduced his look-to-camera which had been missing from most of the Fox films.

Classic Dialogue: Aunt Sophie (on her dead husbands): "I took them all for better or worse..." Ollie: "But not for long!"

Verdict: Included in the book *The 50 Worst Movies Of All Time*, *The Big Noise* is regarded as the poorest of the 1940s movies by Laurel and Hardy fans. 2/5

Nothing But Trouble

Producer BF Zeidman. Screenplay Russell Rouse & Ray Golden. Additional dialogue by Bradford Ropes & Margaret Gruen (uncredited additional material by Buster Keaton). Director Sam Taylor. 69 minutes. Written July-August 1943. Filmed August 1943. Released by MGM, March 1945. With Mary Boland, Henry O'Neill, David Leland

Working Title: The Home Front

Story: Stan and Ollie befriend a young boy, unaware that he is the King of Orlandia. When they find out the truth, they are hired as Chef and Butler by the King's Uncle Saul, who is secretly planning to dispose of the boy. In the end it all works out happily - Uncle Saul accidentally poisons himself before any real damage can be done.

Production: MGM ignored the boys' unique characters and thrust unsuitable dialogue into their mouths. Even with a contribution from Buster Keaton (but none from Laurel or Hardy), the script fails to come to life. Director Sam Taylor had worked with Harold Lloyd, which explains the hair-raising, high-rise climax. Most reviewers agreed with *The New York Times* when it called Laurel and Hardy 'old time' comedians.

Classic Dialogue: Stan: "I have as much right to be as ignorant as you are. In fact, more."

Verdict: It has its moments, but *Nothing But Trouble* is another misfire, forcing Stan and Ollie out of character and into hackneyed comedy conventions. 2/5

The Bullfighters

Producer William Girard. Screenplay W Scott Darling (& Stan Laurel, uncredited). Director Malcolm St Clair (& Stan Laurel, uncredited). 61 minutes. Written mid-late 1944. Filmed November-December 1944. Released by 20th Century-Fox, May 1945. With Richard Lane, Ralph Sanford, Diosa Costello

Story: In Mexico, Detectives Stan and Ollie are on the trail of Larceny Nell, but they get distracted by a gangster caper. Stan's remarkable resemblance to Don Sebastian, the great bullfighter, complicates things.

Production: To acknowledge the success of Laurel and Hardy in Mexico, 20th Century-Fox set the film south of the border. Producer Sol Wurtzel retired and replacement William Girard had little interest in what Laurel and Hardy were up to, as long as their film was on time and budget. As a result, director St Clair gave Stan Laurel more creative control, particularly on the egg fight (recreated from *Hollywood Party*) and the fountain tit-for-tat sequence. The boys even ad libbed. The climax of the film was ruined, however, through the use of stock footage from newsreels of a stadium riot and excerpts from the 1941 Fox film *Blood And Sand*, intercut with Laurel and Hardy looking scared.

The Bullfighters was the final Laurel and Hardy Fox film. Although they only made six films, instead of the 10 asked for, the five-year term of the contract had expired. Despite these poor films, classic Laurel and Hardy were very much in the public eye, with successful cinema re-releases of films like *Saps At Sea*, *Beau Hunks*, *Sons Of The Desert* and *Pardon Us*. When offered a further five-year contract by Fox, Laurel and Hardy declined. They said it was because of Hardy's ill-health and their overseas stage commitments. In reality the boys had finally had enough of the Fox way of making films.

Classic Dialogue: Stan: "I don't want to walk around in my bones!"

Verdict: Now the songs are in Mexican! Diosa Costello was cast after the producer saw her in a nightclub, and she's completely out of place. There's some classic Stan Laurel in this, but it's too little, too late to make any difference. 2/5

Atoll K

Producer Raymond Eger. Screenplay John Klorer, Frederick Kohner, Rene Wheeler & Pierro Tellini. Director Leo Joannon. 98 minutes. Written 1950. Filmed August 1950-March 1951. Released: *Atoll K* (Les Films Serius, France, 1951), 98 minutes; *Robinson Crusoeland* (Franco-London Films, UK, 1952), 82 minutes; *Utopia* (Exploitation Productions, US, 1954), 82 minutes. With Suzy Delair, Max Ellroy, Adriano Rimoldi, Luigi Tosi

Working Titles: Entente Cordiale, Atoll

Story: Travelling to their newly-inherited island, Stan and Ollie, along with a stateless chef and a stowaway, are shipwrecked on a different island (christened Atoll K) rich with Uranium. Ollie declares the island a lawless paradise and himself President. When people start flocking to this utopia, Ollie is thrown out of office and he and Stan are set to be hanged. A storm sinks Atoll K and Stan and Ollie get to their inherited island, where all their possessions are seized by the taxman.

Production: Laurel divorced Ruth and married Ida, a China-born, Russian-descended Opera singer. This match lasted for almost 20 years, until his death. Hardy had further alimony troubles with Myrtle.

Laurel and Hardy returned to the stage, embarking on a six-week tour of the UK (it actually lasted seven months such was their popularity) followed by a tour of Europe. Plans by Laurel to film a version of Robin Hood came to nothing. While Laurel was ill with diabetes, Hardy featured as John Wayne's sidekick in *The Fighting Kentuckian* (1949) and in a humorous cameo in Frank Capra's *Riding High* (1950). These roles showed that Hardy could have pursued a career as a character actor without Laurel, but in deference to his long-term professional partner and his declining health, he didn't seek out any further opportunities.

Five years after their last screen appearance, a consortium of British, French and Italian film producers offered Stan and Ollie *Atoll K*. They were so flattered and tempted by the offer that they put health worries to one side to make the movie in Europe. This Euro-pudding was scripted by Hardy's golf partner John Klorer, American Kohner, Frenchman Wheeler and Italian Tellini: it's no wonder the film is incomprehensible. The Italians wanted a financial and political satire, the French wanted a farce and the Americans seemed to have lost the knack of making Laurel and Hardy comedies. The finished script was rejected by Stan Laurel, but filming was scheduled to go ahead, so he and Hardy had to make the best of it. Adding to their difficulties was the need to act in English opposite a multinational cast all talking in their own languages (and badly dubbed into English for the final film).

During the troubled filming, which extended from 12 weeks to almost a year, both Laurel and Hardy fell ill, mainly due to that summer's heatwave. Hardy suffered from an irregular heartbeat and Laurel was hospitalised due to weight loss, dysentery and prostrate trouble. Laurel looks terrible in the finished film. Despite these troubles, the boys felt duty-bound to finish the film. Filming wrapped in the spring of 1951 and they returned to the US to recover their health and forget the ordeal, under the impression that the film would only be released in Europe and not the US.

Other film offers came but were rejected: *Two Tickets To Broadway* from Howard Hughes at RKO; a biopic from Billy Wilder; a Japanese studio and an Italian film company who wanted Laurel and Hardy in a version of *Carmen*.

Classic Dialogue: Ollie: "Where are we?" Stan: "We're here!"; Stan recommends that Ollie needs glasses, "You'd better see an optomist."

Verdict: Torture to make and torture to watch. If you want to remember Laurel and Hardy in their 1930s prime, just ignore *Atoll K*. There are precious few laughs and the boys appearance will break your heart... A very unfitting finale, despite the classic "Another fine mess" line and Cuckoo Song at the fade-out. 0/5

12. Legacy Of Laughter

The dismal experience of *Atoll K* brought Laurel and Hardy's film careers to an end. By the time of its unexpected US release in 1954, Laurel was 64 and Hardy was 62. Both were in poor health and simply not capable of doing the comic pratfalls that had made them famous. They still worked together, triumphantly touring Britain several times between 1951 and 1953, always to a rapturous welcome. After these tours and with little prospect of future film work, Laurel and Hardy decided in November 1954 to formally retire.

There was one more surprise appearance awaiting the boys: the 1 December 1954 edition of *This Is Your Life*. Brought together by their lawyer Ben Shipman for a meeting with their British tour promoter Bernard Delfont, Laurel and Hardy were surprised to be press-ganged into an unexpected live television appearance. So reluctant was Laurel to appear that a delay was caused to the show, resulting in embarrassed host Ralph Edwards desperately filling airtime. The show itself doesn't amount to much and it was to be the last most people would see of Laurel and Hardy as themselves.

However, the characters of Stan and Babe were widely seen during the 1950s and onwards thanks to television. Producer Hal Roach was one of the first independent film-makers to license the use of his films for the new medium which was seen as a rival to cinema. As a result, the classic Laurel and Hardy shorts of the late-1920s and 1930s found a whole new audience. Often the films were re-edited for television, cut from 20 minutes to 15, much to the consternation of Stan Laurel. Home projection also took off, with many Laurel and Hardy films available on 16mm, 8mm and Super-8 formats for collectors.

The success of the films on television resulted in Hal Roach Jr. approaching Laurel and Hardy to produce a television sitcom. Neither man was interested in the workload involved, but Laurel did begin work on a series of four one-hour colour specials for NBC to be called *Laurel And Hardy's Fabulous Fables*, based on retelling of famous fairy tales, but featuring Stan and Ollie. Planned for the 1956 television season, work on the script progressed slowly, mainly due to the ill-health of the stars.

Stan Laurel suffered a stroke, from which he slowly recovered, while Oliver Hardy was on a diet to reduce his weight and alleviate the heart problems which had troubled him on and off for many years. It didn't work and early on the morning of 14 September 1956 Hardy suffered a massive heart attack. Paralysed, he survived for almost a year, dying at home in North Hollywood, with his wife Lucille by his side, on 7 August 1957, aged 65.

Oliver Hardy's death put paid to any further plans to revive the Laurel and Hardy partnership. Laurel was still bitter about their treatment by Fox and MGM in the 1940s, but they had both been delighted by their new TV audience (although the stars received no payment). Laurel lived out his last few years in an ocean-front apartment in Santa Monica with his wife Ida, replying to thousands of letters of fan mail and entertaining visitors. One was writer and fan John McCabe who proposed writing a biography of Laurel and Hardy, a project to which Laurel happily contributed. The pair also developed the idea for the Sons Of The Desert, a club for friends who liked the movies – this later grew into an international Laurel and Hardy appreciation society.

In 1961 the Academy awarded Stan Laurel an Honorary Oscar for his lifetime contribution to movies. Laurel's only regret was that Hardy was not alive to share in the award. Laurel died from stroke on 23 February 1965, aged 74. With the passing of both Laurel and Hardy, the world lost two of its greatest laughter-makers.

Their legacy of laughter lives on. Film-maker Robert Youngson did much to revive appreciation for the work of Laurel and Hardy through compilation films *The Golden Age Of Comedy* (1958), *Laurel And Hardy's Laughing 20s* (1965) and *The Further Perils of Laurel And Hardy* (1967). Hal Roach joined in with the 1965 compilation *The Crazy World Of Laurel And Hardy*. A 1960s Hanna-Barbera television cartoon series used the likenesses of Stan and Ollie, drawn by Larry Harmon. Television screenings have continued over the years and new generations of fans can now collect almost every available film on video and DVD.

Whatever image storage formats or methods of broadcasting or distribution might develop in the future, we can be sure of one thing: Laurel and Hardy will always be there to bring laughter to new generations, hundreds of years after they created the comedy icons of Stan and Ollie.

13. Reference Materials

Books

If you want to know more about Laurel & Hardy, I can heartily recommend the following books (most of them consulted in writing this work):

Mr Laurel And Mr Hardy, John McCabe, Robson Books, 1976
The Comedy World Of Stan Laurel, John McCabe, Robson Books, 1975
Babe: The Life Of Oliver Hardy, John McCabe, Robson Books, 1977
The Laurel & Hardy Encyclopædia, Glenn Mitchell, Batsford, 1995
Another Fine Dress, Jonathan Sanders, Cassell, 1995, 2000
The Complete Films Of Laurel & Hardy, William K Everson, Citadel Press, 1967, 1995
Laurel And Hardy: The Magic Behind The Movies, Randy Skretvedt, Past Times Publishing, 1987, 1996
Laurel & Hardy In "Big Quizness," Robert & Tracie McFerren, Plumtree Publishing, 1997
Laurel & Hardy: From The Forties Forward, Scott MacGillivray, Vestal Press, 1998

Sons Of The Desert

The International Laurel and Hardy Appreciation Society. Local branches are called tents and are named after Laurel and Hardy films, such as the Bonnie Scotland tent in Glasgow. Fans gather for social evenings and film screenings. Many publish magazines.

Sons Of The Desert, PO Box 36, Almelund, MN 55002, USA
Sons Of The Desert, 102 Hough Green Road, Widnes, Cheshire, WA8 9PF, UK

Websites

http://www.sotd.org/ – Sons Of The Desert
http://www.laurel-and-hardy.com/html/links.html – Official Homepage
http://www.geocities.com/Hollywood/Academy/4706/ – The Another Fine Mess tent
http://www.geocities.com/Hollywood/Cinema/6141/ – The Intra-Tent Journal
http://members.aol.com/oxford0614/ – Laurel and Hardy Memorabilia
http://www.liveghost.com/ – The Live Ghost London tent
http://freespace.virgin.net/bowler.dessert/ – Bowler Desert Magazine
http://www.uno.edu/~drcom/Slapstick/SlapLH.html – Laurel and Hardy Quicktime clips

The Essential Library

Build up your library with new titles every month

New This Month:

Laurel & Hardy (£3.99)   **Marx Brothers** (£3.99)

Film Directors:

Jane Campion (£2.99)	**John Carpenter** (£3.99)
Jackie Chan (£2.99)	**Joel & Ethan Coen** (£3.99)
David Cronenberg (£3.99)	**Terry Gilliam** (£2.99)
Alfred Hitchcock (£3.99)	**Krzysztof Kieslowski** (£2.99)
Stanley Kubrick (£2.99)	**Sergio Leone** (£3.99)
David Lynch (£3.99)	**Brian De Palma** (£2.99)
Sam Peckinpah (£2.99)	**Ridley Scott** (£3.99)
Orson Welles (£2.99)	**Billy Wilder** (£3.99)
Woody Allen (£3.99)	**Steven Spielberg** (£3.99)

Film Genres:

Film Noir (£3.99)	**Hong Kong Heroic Bloodshed** (£2.99)
Horror Films (£3.99)	**Slasher Movies**(£3.99)
Spaghetti Westerns (£3.99)	**Vampire Films** (£2.99)
Blaxploitation Films (£3.99)	

Film Subjects:

Steve McQueen (£2.99)	**Marilyn Monroe** (£3.99)
The Oscars® (£3.99)	**Filming On A Microbudget** (£3.99)
Bruce Lee (£3.99)	

TV:

Doctor Who (£3.99)

Literature:

Cyberpunk (£3.99)	**Philip K Dick** (£3.99)
Hitchhiker's Guide (£3.99)	**Noir Fiction** (£2.99)
Terry Pratchett (£3.99)	**Sherlock Holmes** (£3.99)

Ideas:

Conspiracy Theories (£3.99)	**Nietzsche** (£3.99)
Feminism (£3.99)	

History:

Alchemy & Alchemists (£3.99) **The Crusades** (£3.99)

Available at all good bookstores, or send a cheque to: **Pocket Essentials (Dept LH), 18 Coleswood Rd, Harpenden, Herts, AL5 1EQ, UK**. Please make cheques payable to 'Oldcastle Books.' Add 50p postage & packing for each book in the UK and £1 elsewhere.

US customers can send $6.95 plus $1.95 postage & packing for each book to: **Trafalgar Square Publishing, PO Box 257, Howe Hill Road, North Pomfret, Vermont 05053, USA**. e-mail: tsquare@sover.net

Customers worldwide can order online at **www.pocketessentials.com**.